CAMBRIDGE LIBRARY COLLECTION

Books of enduring scholarly value

Egyptology

The large-scale scientific investigation of Egyptian antiquities by Western scholars began as an unintended consequence of Napoleon's invasion of Egypt during which, in 1799, the Rosetta Stone was discovered. The military expedition was accompanied by French scholars, whose reports prompted a wave of enthusiasm that swept across Europe and North America resulting in the Egyptian Revival style in art and architecture. Increasing numbers of tourists visited Egypt, eager to see the marvels being revealed by archaeological excavation. Writers and booksellers responded to this growing interest with publications ranging from technical site reports to tourist guidebooks and from children's histories to theories identifying the pyramids as repositories of esoteric knowledge. This series reissues a wide selection of such books. They reveal the gradual change from the 'tomb-robbing' approach of early excavators to the highly organised and systematic approach of Flinders Petrie, the 'father of Egyptology', and include early accounts of the decipherment of the hieroglyphic script.

Egyptian History and Art

The Egyptologist Annie Quibell, née Pirie (1862–1927) became a student of Sir Flinders Petrie, copying wall-paintings and inscriptions at his Saqqara excavations, where she met her husband, who was an inspector for the Egyptian Antiquities Service. Accompanying him and sharing in his work on site, she was keen to popularise the marvels of ancient Egyptian civilisation, writing several works for the lay reader. This 1923 book is a new edition of a work originally focusing on the Cairo Museum, but now intended as a historical guide to Egyptian collections in general. She advises that it should be skimmed through before any visit, 'sufficiently to get an impression of the great length of Egyptian history', but can also be used afterwards to follow up any particular interest. The very recent discovery of Tutankhamen's tomb, 'just as the book was going to press', enthuses Quibell with prospects for the future.

Cambridge University Press has long been a pioneer in the reissuing of out-of-print titles from its own backlist, producing digital reprints of books that are still sought after by scholars and students but could not be reprinted economically using traditional technology. The Cambridge Library Collection extends this activity to a wider range of books which are still of importance to researchers and professionals, either for the source material they contain, or as landmarks in the history of their academic discipline.

Drawing from the world-renowned collections in the Cambridge University Library and other partner libraries, and guided by the advice of experts in each subject area, Cambridge University Press is using state-of-the-art scanning machines in its own Printing House to capture the content of each book selected for inclusion. The files are processed to give a consistently clear, crisp image, and the books finished to the high quality standard for which the Press is recognised around the world. The latest print-on-demand technology ensures that the books will remain available indefinitely, and that orders for single or multiple copies can quickly be supplied.

The Cambridge Library Collection brings back to life books of enduring scholarly value (including out-of-copyright works originally issued by other publishers) across a wide range of disciplines in the humanities and social sciences and in science and technology.

Egyptian History and Art

With Reference to Museum Collections

ANNIE ABERNETHIE PIRIE QUIBELL

CAMBRIDGE
UNIVERSITY PRESS

CAMBRIDGE
UNIVERSITY PRESS

University Printing House, Cambridge, CB2 8BS, United Kingdom

Cambridge University Press is part of the University of Cambridge.
It furthers the University's mission by disseminating knowledge in the pursuit of
education, learning and research at the highest international levels of excellence.

www.cambridge.org
Information on this title: www.cambridge.org/9781108081962

© in this compilation Cambridge University Press 2018

This edition first published 1923
This digitally printed version 2018

ISBN 978-1-108-08196-2 Paperback

EGYPTIAN HISTORY AND ART

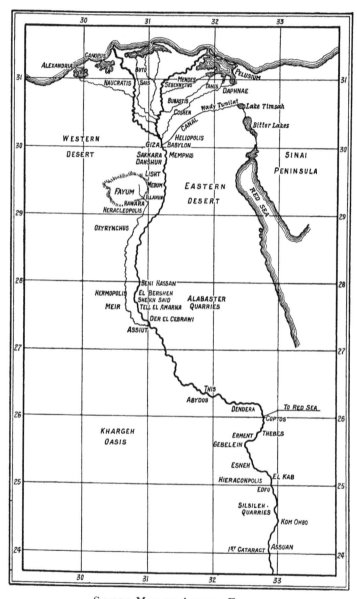

SKETCH MAP OF ANCIENT EGYPT.

EGYPTIAN
HISTORY AND ART

WITH REFERENCE TO MUSEUM
COLLECTIONS

BY

MRS. A. A. QUIBELL

WITH MAP AND ILLUSTRATIONS

LONDON
SOCIETY FOR PROMOTING
CHRISTIAN KNOWLEDGE
NEW YORK AND TORONTO : THE MACMILLAN CO.

1923

PREFACE

MOST of this little history was published a few years ago with reference especially to the Cairo Museum, and it has been found useful by so many people that I am encouraged to hope that it may be of service as an historical guide to Egyptian collections in general.

The book should be used both before and after visiting museums; in the first place, it should be at least skimmed over sufficiently to get an impression of the great length of Egyptian history and the divisions into which it naturally falls, while afterwards special periods can be read up as required. Almost all large collections are in some sort of chronological order so far as the limitations of space and the weight of objects permit, but in small museums it is generally impossible to separate out Egyptian objects one from the other enough to show the sequence; moreover, there are apt to be periods quite unrepresented, but if the descriptions and illustrations are gone through with some care, a foundation at least will be laid for seeing Egyptian things intelligently, so that on looking at any object we may have some idea why and when it was made.

The present edition has been brought up to date in every particular, though the great discovery of the tomb of Tutankhamen just as the book was going to press is a signal warning against making too cut-and-dry statements. This tomb has aroused such extraordinary interest that I regret very much the impossibility of giving any detailed description of the objects, and it will be a long time before the entire contents can be seen by the public; but the newspaper articles have been so full and the official accounts so good that people are actually much better acquainted with the furniture of Tutankhamen, which they have only seen from pictures, than with any of the furniture in museums, which they might have seen at any time.

As soon as the burial chamber was opened it became evident that the work must be shut down and the tomb closed until the winter. It will take the excavators the remainder of this season—already far advanced—to finish the treatment and packing of the vast mass of material found in the two outer chambers, and it is to be hoped that the finest of these things will be shown in the Cairo Museum by the autumn of 1923. When the tomb is reopened there will come the serious mechanical difficulties of examining and taking to pieces the huge catafalque or canopy which nearly fills the funeral chamber and undoubtedly contains the mummy of the king, enclosed in one or two other canopies and probably two or three splendid coffins. There is also, in a small adjoining room, a large amount of funeral furniture of the kind specially belonging to the ritual for the dead, a great Canopic chest with protecting deities guarding it at the four corners, *ushabtiu* figures, statues, and other objects. The unparalleled interest and importance of it lies in the fact that this is the first practically undisturbed royal tomb that has ever been found. By the greatest good fortune the staff of experts who are employed upon it are the very best possible, and the reward of their labour will be that for all time to come archæologists, historians, and artists will recognise that the best that could be done for them has been done, that every record that could be taken has been taken, and so, in a very full sense, this magnificent discovery will remain a possession for posterity.

In the preparation of the book I wish to express my sincere thanks to Dr. Reisner and Professor Breasted for their assistance, to Sir Ernest Budge and the Trustees of the British Museum for permission to publish the stela of Rahotep, to Mr. A. M. Lythgoe and the authorities of the Metropolitan Museum for photographs of the *mastaba* of Perneb and of three of the models from the "First Dark Period," and lastly to Mr. J. E. Quibell, Keeper of the Cairo Museum, for all the other photographic illustrations, as well as for much advice and information.

ANNIE A. QUIBELL.

CONTENTS

ix

LIST OF ILLUSTRATIONS

IN THE TEXT

PLATES AT END OF BOOK

xi

EGYPTIAN HISTORY AND ART

CHAPTER I

EARLIEST EGYPT

(3500 B.C.)

THE earliest history of European nations, the history we learned in our childhood, lies enveloped in a mist of legend to which the poetry of later ages has lent form and substance. A glory is shed about the life of a hero or the founding of a city, and when the drier annals of recorded events take the place of the ancient tales, they in turn are gradually clothed by literature with the character in which they live for us. When, for instance, we see or read of the discoveries of the oldest Rome in the Forum or the Palatine, or when we go to see Westminster Abbey or Windsor Castle, it is not so much the beauty of what we see that impresses us, but that we remember what we learned about the beginnings of Rome, the legends of Romulus and the early kings; and that in Windsor and Westminster we have treasure houses full of memorials of our own English past—in other words, we are interested in these things chiefly because we know the stories about them.

It is otherwise with Egypt. Very few tales or legends of ancient Egypt have been preserved and such as there are have no associations for us, so our interest in Egyptian history must come from another side altogether; we must work back from the things to the people, from the

I

I

art to the artists.   And this is a somewhat difficult and discouraging task, for where there is very little literature and an enormous amount of things, the human interest is apt to be overwhelmed under masses of museum specimens.   Some Egyptian monuments, however, are so impressive from their very vastness and magnificence that they have taken great hold of the imagination of mankind, while on the other hand if, by a rare chance, we can look into an undisturbed tomb and see the offerings lying as they were placed there thousands of years ago, even the humblest of offerings and the poorest of burials has power to send a thrill through the beholder. That, it may be said, is quite true : most people can appreciate the splendour of the Pyramids or Karnak and most would have enough imagination to like to be the first to look into an ancient tomb " and in a corner find the toys of the old Egyptian boys "—but as to looking at these same toys shut up in a museum case out of their surroundings, away from anything that makes them intelligible, can this be anything but a dreary waste of time for modern men and women ?

It is indeed difficult and needs sustained effort to keep the human side of " antiquities " before our minds; and to many people the appeal is not strong, but to many others these Egyptian objects, in themselves so curious, often so beautiful and undoubtedly so old, have a great power to compel and retain attention, all the more perhaps that there is an element of uncertainty about many of them, that they are continually setting problems, the answers to which may be found any day or may even already be lying before us undetected.   From another point of view also the history and archæology of Egypt have an importance for modern life, for there we find the first steps in human civilisation.   Egypt not only has by far the oldest art in the world, but possesses the earliest specimens of almost every handicraft, such as writing, weaving, ceramics, and every student of ancient culture must turn to Egypt for the beginnings of his subject.   But it is all fragmentary and very remote, and has to be pieced together like a puzzle from the scanty remains that have escaped destruction.

For the early periods the case is worst of all, for not only, as is natural, must we reconstruct as best we may from the objects without any literature at all to help us, but there is a further and most serious limitation in the fact that practically everything that has come down to us comes from graves, and so, though we may be tolerably well informed about the funeral customs of the most ancient inhabitants, we may be very much astray about their everyday lives. The reason for this is inevitable from the character of the country. Men always lived on the narrow strip of cultivated land, built their houses of its mud as they do to-day, and the next generation built after them on the crumbling brick ruins or ran the plough over them and built somewhere else. In either case, furniture, written scrolls, almost all that was used by the living, has perished.

The sites of many of the towns are marked by mounds of mud brick which are dotted about over the whole country: that of Memphis in particular, is crossed by everyone who goes to Sakkara from Bedrashein station. These mounds used to be much higher than they now are, as was to be expected from the practice of building one house on the ruins of another, but, unluckily for the antiquities, the organic refuse known as *sebakh* which they contain has valuable fertilising properties and the peasants are allowed to remove it—under some slight restriction—to use as manure. In such mounds and in this way many things are found, usually objects of pottery or metal which have escaped destruction from damp, and the collections of small antiquities to be seen in dealers' shops generally come from this source; but such things, even when valuable in themselves, rarely give any historical information, as no one is ever sure how or exactly where they were found.

But in towns there were not only the perishable houses of men; there were temples to the gods, built of massive blocks of stone and filled with every sort of treasure;

there, if anywhere, one might think we should look for historical records. For the most ancient times, however, these are totally lacking. The oldest temples, such as that of Ra of Heliopolis and Ptah of Memphis, have entirely disappeared, and though there are very important inscriptions at Karnak and in some of the mortuary temples at Thebes, these come from a comparatively late period of the history, while the best preserved of the temples, Edfu, Dendera, and others, date from the times of the Ptolemaic and Roman rulers. All the temples were, of course, plundered long ages ago, but by one or two rare strokes of good fortune, some of the treasures hidden in ancient times have come to light in recent years. These will be noticed in due course, but in the meantime it must be repeated that the sources for early Egyptian history and for knowledge of old Egyptian life come almost exclusively from the graves; for from time immemorial the graves were on the high, dry desert, where the land cost nothing and where, if thieves did not break through and steal, moth and rust and other corruption were not much to be feared. Right along the whole Nile Valley from the Sudan to the sea, there stretches a line of cemetery, irregular on the east side but on the west almost unbroken, for the dead followed the setting sun to rest on the western horizon.

The tombs were always robbed; in old times for jewellery and fine carved stones, in modern times for anything that can be sold to collectors, and it is from the scanty leavings of the former robbers that the last of the race, the archæologist, the scientific robber in search of facts, has to piece together his bits of evidence. He alone, at least, feels his responsibility to the future for what he is doing; he knows that when things have once been moved out of place the testimony they can give is lost unless it has been noted with the utmost care. His clear duty is to record everything he sees, however insignificant it may seem; his unpardonable sin is omission or neglect.

It is by such faithful following out of the testimony

of things that a considerable amount of knowledge has
been arrived at about the earliest civilisation of the Nile
Valley, as disclosed by the oldest graves and the offerings
that were placed in them, but before beginning a review
of these it is well to try to realise their enormous antiquity
and also the fact that they lie far beyond any other
known remains, so that there is no collateral history by
which their age can be checked. The civilisation of
Mesopotamia may be as old, but it is not till many ages
have passed that there is any sureness of contemporary
dating. Long and lonely, like its river, the story of
Egypt flows on, a narrow strip of civilised life among
boundless wastes of desert, and it is only far on in its
course that it mingles with the tides of changing peoples
that surround the Mediterranean shores. At the very
dawn of our English history, when the Roman legions
first set foot in Britain, Egypt's independence was gone
for ever, and we must go back beyond Rome, beyond the
great ages of Greece and even of Mycenæ to get level
with a time when Egypt was really a queen among the
nations; while before that there had been nearly two
thousand years of glory and decay, and yet again of rise
and fall of her power, since the time when Menes joined
the kingdoms of Upper and Lower Egypt under one
rule and founded his town of Memphis. It should be
said, too, that this leaves out of account the far more
ancient remains of palæolithic man, which belong, in all
probability, to an epoch when the geologic condition
and climate of the country were different from what they
became in historic times. The Cairo Museum contains
a good collection of these flint implements, which are
found in large numbers on the high desert plateau in
Upper Egypt.

Beginning then with Egypt, the gift of the Nile, as
Herodotus called it—as it was at the dawn of history,
and as it is to-day, an abundantly fertile strip drenched
yearly by the life-giving flood and bounded by vast
solitudes of rock and sand—at the earliest dim past we
can discern the rule held good that men lived on the

good ground and were buried on the desert. They made very simple graves, just a small shallow pit in which the body was laid, not at full length but crouching, with knees bent and hands before the face. But even these little graves can give us answers to some of the questions we want to ask. If we go round the archaic room, or the cases containing archaic objects, in any museum, we shall see the things which were put into the graves along with the bodies—pottery and stone jars, flint tools, beads, slate palettes, scraps of ivory. These jars were to hold food and drink, the flint knives were to cut up meat, the palette with a lump of green paint beside it was to mix face paint, the beads were for ornament; but the real significance of all these things for the use of the dead is that it shows that these people believed that the dead had needs, that the death of the body was not the end, but that some part, at least, of a man's personality went on into a future life.

Reconstructions of such graves are to be seen in a good many museums.

In the British Museum the prehistoric burial is placed as the earliest of the series of coffins, which are, as far as possible, chronologically arranged, but the objects found in such graves are mostly in wall cases in the Sixth Room. In American museums, where more space is available, a special room has generally been arranged, so that the prehistoric burial is placed along with the other objects of the period.

The things in themselves are well worthy of notice, for the flints are among the finest ever made. They and the very decorative shapes and designs of the pottery will prepare us for the great skill in artistic handiwork that came later. The pottery is all hand-made; the invention of the potter's wheel only came in about the beginning of the historic period, but later pottery is seldom so attractive as these very early products. The slate palettes, which are very often found, point to a practice of outlining the eyes with green or black paint, traces of which are to be noted in later times. The large number of ceremonial flints, knives, etc., indicates a scarcity of metal, or ignorance of how to use it, but it is somewhat surprising to find that gold and copper do occur in minute quantities, even in the oldest tombs.

A good deal that is interesting has been found out from careful examination of the bodies, some of which are preserved in the College of Surgeons, London, and other anatomical museums. There is no sign of mummification, but the preservation of some of these bodies is remarkable, skin, hair, and all the internal organs having been found, dried up indeed, but perfectly recognisable after 6,000 or 7,000 years. It has often been said that the Egyptian race was a blend of several different stocks and influenced by invaders from east, south, and west. It may be so, but the anatomical evidence shows that the oldest peasant inhabitant of the Nile Valley was, in build and stature, very much like the fellah of to-day. Probably the race had always a capacity for absorbing foreign elements.

A curious fact given to us by the anatomical observers is that the prehistoric people suffered dreadfully from rheumatism and rheumatoid arthritis, some of their bones being shapeless and distorted from this disease and the great majority were affected by it, a condition that is never known in later times, though occasional cases of arthritis occur at any period; and this agrees very well with what we might expect at a time when the inundation must have swept over all the country, with no regulation by sluices or dykes. People must have lived in damp mud and undrained marshes for a great part of the year —not much wonder they had rheumatism! Before leaving the question of the skeletons of the early Egyptians, another small point has been observed—namely, that in some cemeteries the women habitually have their left forearm broken. The only explanation as yet suggested for this is that they got them broken by endeavouring to protect their heads from the blows of their male relatives, and one hesitates to attribute such unpleasant conduct to people who could make such delightful pottery. The fact and the conjecture are merely stated as specimens of the unexpected difficulties which may confront the archæologist.

No date, even approximate, can be assigned to these graves. It is safe to consider them as before 4000 B.C., but many of them must be much older than that. Unfortunately the cemeteries have only been found in Upper Egypt, where the extreme dryness of the climate preserves everything, and it is much more difficult to know anything about the Delta, which is damp in comparison and where the people lived so far from the desert that they must needs bury their dead in the cultivated land, therefore all trace of their graves is irretrievably lost. But it is certain that civilisation developed there at least as early as in the south, for the few records which exist show that there were temples to the gods and dynasties of kings in Lower as well as Upper Egypt before Menes, and there is good reason to believe that the art of writing and the regulation of the calendar, both of which were probably introduced before 4000 B.C., were the work of the priests of Ra of Heliopolis. The great superiority of the Egyptian to all other ancient calendars lies in the fact that the Egyptians had a fixed and most important point by which to measure time, for the Nile flood and not the changes of the moon, was the phenomenon which must have influenced them the most. They observed that the appearance of Sirius above the horizon at sunrise closely corresponded with the beginning of the inundation In the latitude of Heliopolis the rising of Sirius takes place, by our dating, on July 19, and this day was accordingly chosen as the Egyptian New Year's Day, the first of the month of Thoth. The year was divided into three seasons—the flood, the spring, and the harvest; each month had thirty days and there were five extra or "intercalary" days added at the end of the year, making a total of 365 days, a very good calculation for ordinary purposes and for one generation. But the want of a leap year gradually got the seasons very badly wrong, the inundation months slipped back to the harvest, and so on, losing one day in every four years, till after 1,460 years it came right once more and Sirius again rose on the first of Thoth. The Egyptians knew about this fault in their reckoning quite well, and the astronomical check which can be given to some dates in the history is most valuable, for if an inscription happens to mention the month and day of the month on which the rising of Sirius is due, the date can then be computed to within four years. Unluckily such mentions are very rare; the most important of them will be noted in due course.

The earliest indications which have come down to us regarding the state of the country show Egypt divided into two kingdoms, the north and the south, but it is highly probable that at a still more remote period there were numbers of local or tribal chiefs. The oldest chronicle of Egyptian history is a fragment of inscription on a block of black stone in the Palermo Museum, generally known as the Palermo Stone. Some chips from a duplicate copy exist in Cairo. This is a list of kings drawn up in the Fifth Dynasty (about 2700 B.C.), when there was a long line of unbroken tradition and doubtless many written records to go upon, and if it had only been a little more complete the names at least of the early kings would have been preserved. As it is, nine kings who reigned in Lower Egypt before Menes are recorded. Their capital was Buto in the Delta, of which town practically nothing remains, but the southern capital, Hieraconpolis or Nekhen, is in somewhat better preservation.

The centuries that preceded the union of the two kingdoms under Menes saw considerable changes in the burial customs from what has been noted in regard to the primitive graves. Rich men began to make more and more elaborate tombs, the shallow pit became a deep shaft, an inner chamber was hollowed out to contain the body, the walls were bricklined, the offerings were more abundant and costly. Altogether there is evidence of an increase in prosperity which must surely have been

brought about by a regulation of the water supply, for
that has always been the first necessity of Egypt, and
there is every reason to believe that before the time of
Menes an irrigation system, demanding a regular supply
of labour on a large scale and considerable mechanical
skill, was well established throughout the country. The
effect of such a measure can hardly be over-estimated,
involving, as it would do, power vested in some one or
more chiefs to call up disciplined labour when required
to dig canals and raise dykes. This was a great stride
towards a centralised government and a civilised community.

We cannot leave even this very brief account of the
earliest state of Egypt without a reference to its religion.
The study of all early religion is beset with difficulties
and that of Egypt is no exception, although one or two
leading ideas may be traced throughout its history.
There were local gods in bewildering numbers, but,
through the confusion of myths and the grotesqueness of
some of the legends, there stand out even from the most
remote antiquity two great powers of nature which were
worshipped by all Egypt, at all times, in one form or
another, and these were the two we should reasonably
look for in such a land—the sun and the Nile. The
earliest mythology shows us these as Ra and Osiris,
the earliest sanctuaries at Heliopolis and Abydos, and
through all changes, additions, and interfusions, we shall
find some sort of guidance if we keep these two in mind
—Ra, the heavenly king, source of all power and glory;
and Osiris, the life-giving, recurring flood, god of the
springing corn and the gathered harvest, lord of death
and resurrection.

CHAPTER II

PART I.—EARLY DYNASTIES

(3500–3000 B.C.)

THE beginning of Egyptian history may be reckoned from the reign of Menes, when, after a long past of independent development, the kingdoms of the north and the south were united under one sovereign. As the only contemporary record of this event comes from the south, we should be led from it to believe that the union was a triumph of Upper Egypt over Lower, that a victorious king of the south acquired lordship over a conquered Delta; but the testimony of all subsequent history goes to show that it was a union on perfectly equal terms The Egyptians were so conservative in their ways of thinking and so full of reverence for their past that the fact of there having originally been two kingdoms was never lost sight of; the king was always entitled " lord of the two lands," the symbolic flowers of the north and the south were entwined upon the throne of the Pharaohs, while the reed sign of Upper Egypt and the bee sign of Lower Egypt preceded the royal name on every proclamation.

The most important object belonging to this early period is a large, shield-like carved slate which stands in a case by itself in the archaic room of the Cairo Museum. It is one of the exceptional things that were not found in tombs. This slate formed part of the treasure in the temple of Nekhen or Hieraconpolis, the old capital of Upper Egypt before the union, and what must have happened is that at some much later time, probably from fear of plunder by invaders, this palette, together with a quantity of other objects made at the same early period, and one or two very valuable things dating from about a thousand years later, were all buried in a vault below the temple, where they lay undisturbed until recent times.

SLATE PALETTE FROM HIERACONPOLIS: BACK. (63 cm. long.)

SLATE PALETTE FROM HIERACONPOLIS: FRONT. (63 cm. long.)

This slate is such a fine piece of work and forms so excellent an introduction to the study of historical monuments that it will repay a detailed examination, and it may be selected as a typical specimen of archaic art. Here we may fairly say that we catch Egypt in the act of uniting, for this is almost certainly the work of an immediate predecessor of King Menes, and represents the King of Upper Egypt as having gained a victory over the King of the north. On the one side we see the god Horus, figured as a hawk, bringing in the captives, and facing him the King, who wears the white crown of Upper Egypt and grasps a conquered enemy by the hair. This is the first example of what became the conventional representation of victories, and is to be seen repeated innumerable times on stelæ and on temple walls. He wields a mace with a pear-shaped head, no doubt the weapon in actual use at the time, for in other cases in the same room numbers of similar stone mace-heads are to be seen, which were found at the same time and place, and also model maces made for the use of the dead, which come from tombs of the period.

On the other side of the palette, the King, Narmer, wearing the red crown of Lower Egypt, goes out preceded by standard-bearers to see the field of battle or to inspect the headless corpses of his enemies. Below, in the narrow part of the slate, the space is filled by a representation of the King as a strong bull breaking down the battlements of a fortified town, and although this figurative scene does not often recur, the title of "strong bull" is very frequently ascribed to the King in later times. The circular space in the centre of the palette calls for explanation, but here we have a survival of former days and not a precedent for the future. This indeed is what makes it evident that the object was a palette and not a model shield, for the circle in the middle is the part where the paint was mixed.

Although this is a direct descendant of the slate palettes found in the prehistoric tombs, an object of such size and covered with such fine decoration could only have been made for some special occasion, and there can be little doubt that it was a votive offering to commemorate a victory and that the paint to be mixed on it was the paint with which the face of the divine statue was to be adorned. A similar but smaller palette was found in the same *cache* at Hieraconpolis; it is covered with designs of animals and seems to represent a hunting scene. It is now in the Ashmolean Museum at Oxford.

Let us consider for a little what may be known of Egypt at this remote age. Men had long since cultivated grain and domesticated animals; they lived in brick houses and made boats of wood and papyrus; they had plenty of ivory and even some gold and copper for ornaments; they made beautiful pottery and the finest of flint tools; and now, at the dawn of history, we see that they had attained to extraordinary skill in working small objects of stone; they had evidently begun to regulate the inundation to some extent; they could weave very fine linen; and they had begun to invent a system of writing The cemeteries show (see Map) that there were towns of considerable size at or near Coptos, Gebelein, Silsileh and other places in Upper Egypt, as well as at This, near the modern Girga, which was reputed to be the place of origin of the kings of the first two dynasties. West of it, at Abydos, the god Osiris was believed to have been buried; there, from very early times, was the shrine for his worship, and the whole cemetery was accounted the most sacred spot in all the country. Of the Delta much less is known—little more than the fact that the ancient capital was at Buto and that the temple of Ra of Heliopolis already existed—indeed, was already old

Menes founded a new capital at the junction of the two lands a few miles to the south of where Cairo now is, and soon, with the rise of Memphis, the worship of Ptah the artificer, the local god, became very prominent, and the most important buildings tended to gather round the new centre. Although perhaps a royal residence from the first, Memphis did not become the royal burying-place for some centuries, for the kings of the First and Second Dynasties were buried at Abydos in huge *mastaba* tombs of the old type, which lie a little to the west of the spendid temple in which Seti commemorated them two thousand years later.

By the time of the Third Dynasty, when the royal tomb was moved to Memphis, the country had made immense progress; mankind had possessed themselves of metal in large quantities and could use all the skill that had slowly matured in the manufacture of finely wrought bowls and palettes to hew mighty rocks and dress the hardest of stones wherewith to beautify their temples and graves.

As early as the First Dynasty they had begun to work copper mines in Sinai and have left the records of the work carved on the rocks there; inscriptions in relief with the name of the King and how he smote the Beduin of the desert. Not only that, but Professor Flinders Petrie, in his researches there, even found traces of the workmen's huts and marks of the chisels on the stones, while the pounders by which the ore was crushed, a pottery crucible for pouring out the molten metal and masses of slag, show that the copper was actually smelted at the mines. These mines were worked for more than two thousand years, but their unparalleled interest for us lies in these First-Dynasty records, which mark the opening of a new age for humanity.

Most museums have some objects of this period which are worth study. To be noted are tall food jars with clay sealings, many of which come from the royal tombs of Abydos and have given the names of several of the oldest kings. These jars were filled with grain or wine; if for liquid, they were daubed over inside with pitch, then a pottery lid was put on, a wisp of straw laid over it, and the vase was closed by means of a large cone of unbaked clay, up and down which was rolled a cylinder inscribed with the king's name.

Much more beautiful in workmanship are the ivory implements, spoons, hairpins, pieces for a game, inlay from boxes, and such-like, vases of rock crystal and other costly stone, some of which have been found with their original covering of thick gold leaf tied with string. But perhaps the most remarkable things are in a small case in the jewel room of Cairo Museum. It contains the oldest jewellery in the world, and among this little collection, oldest and most beautiful of all, are four bracelets which belonged to a queen of the First Dynasty and were buried with her in her tomb at Abydos (Plate I. 1). When, afterwards, in all probability very soon afterwards, robbers plundered the tomb and tore the jewels from the dead, so great was their haste that they wrenched off the arm with the bracelets on it, yet did not succeed in getting it away, but hid it in a crevice of the tomb wall, where it stayed and was so found a few years ago, the bracelets still safely fastened on the withered arm The stones and metals employed are gold, lapis-lazuli, carnelian, amethyst, and turquoise, or blue glaze. Strange to say, progress in art at least was not continuous during the five centuries that the first two dynasties lasted, for after the very fine and delicate work which is characteristic of the First Dynasty there is a decided falling off in the Second Dynasty, but possibly this was caused by the introduction of metal tools, which may have induced the craftsmen to set their hands more willingly to bigger and more quickly finished pieces.

The Third Dynasty, however, shows a rapid rise in prosperity, in art, and, so far as can be discerned, a great development in ideas as well, which will be treated of in the second part of this chapter.

A sort of illustrated catalogue of the things in use at this time was found a few years ago in the tomb of Hesy at Sakkara. It is one of the latest of the brick *mastaba* type of tomb, and its existence has been known for over a generation, for out of it came a set of famous wooden panels, which are among the finest of the early objects in Cairo, but the native workmen who extracted these panels from a row of niches along a corridor failed to notice a series of faded but most important paintings on the opposite wall. These pictures are a list of the tomb furniture which was supplied to Hesy on his funeral day; the paintings were, of course, executed during his lifetime and under his direction, and it is a matter of great interest to find the regular shapes of chairs, tables, and bedsteads already well established so early as the Third Dynasty What was not quite well established were the rules of perspective : later Egyptian artists, if they did not exactly see how the four legs of a chair or a bed ought to be drawn, had at least been taught where they were expected to be put in a picture, and a very little

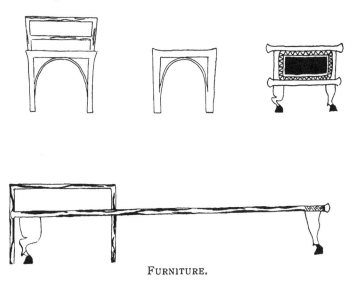

FURNITURE.

practice in looking at Egyptian drawings brings us to accept their conventions quite cheerfully, but, as the line drawing shows, the artist in Hesy's tomb was still a good deal embarrassed by the problem.

It was during the Third Dynasty that the great step was taken of changing from brick to stone in building. The oldest stone erection in the world, the Step Pyramid of Sakkara, rises in sight of Cairo, and another monument of this period is the large unfinished tomb near Zawiyet el Aryan, about an hour's donkey-ride to the south of the Giza pyramids on the way to Sakkara.

Whether it was intended to be a pyramid or a huge *mastaba* is not certain, but the place gives a good idea of the scale on which the preparations for a royal grave were undertaken, and the granite sarcophagus which is already in place, as well as the rough granite blocks of the foundations, all of which must have come from Assuan, show that problems of building and transport had been thoroughly solved before the time of building the Great Pyramid. In fact, by the end of the Third Dynasty, Egypt had completely emerged from the archaic period, and Egyptian art displays absolute mastery over material, and withal a freshness and vigour that is only granted to a nation in its youth.

PART II —DEVELOPMENT OF THE TOMB

During the five or six centuries of the early dynastic period there was, as has been pointed out in the first part of this chapter, a phenomenal progress in all the arts of civilisation. Life in the Nile Valley had changed from primitive, almost barbaric, conditions to those of a highly centralised state, ruled over by a powerful monarch, with a wealthy nobility and various grades of dependents. This is quite certain, but the evidence for it is still mainly found in the cemeteries.

Now, the traveller to Egypt is generally confronted with the graves of this rich and very artistic people at an advanced stage of their development, and, however much he may admire, he can hardly fail to be bewildered by their scheme and decoration. We may read that what is known as a *mastaba* was the plain brick or stone superstructure of a tomb, so called in Arabic because of its likeness to the bench which is to be seen outside old-fashioned Egyptian houses. But what has that to do with the tomb of Ti, or the tomb of Mera, which are also called *mastabas?*

It will not be lost time to try to understand the connection, for it will render the great cemeteries of Giza and Sakkara much more interesting to visit and it will explain the meaning of many museum objects, as well as give the reader the satisfaction of having a reasonable sequence of ideas in his mind.

The regular development has only recently been traced in detail, and the nature of the earliest super-structures has to be taken for granted, as there are none remaining previous to the First Dynasty, but the assumptions made are quite safe, as from the steps taken subsequently, it is clear what the earlier stages must have been. The accompanying diagram (p. 20) will show the changes that took place in the structure of the tomb from its beginning in prehistoric times as a simple hole in the ground with a mound heaped above it. There must always have been some kind of a shelter erected above the mound to hold the food offerings that were brought on the funeral day, and also some rough stones laid about it to mark the place. The first advance on the primitive pit was to line and floor it with brick and to face the mound above with brick also (stage 2 in the diagram), which then indeed began to look very much like a bench, or a small windowless house. Outside of this there was in most, if not in all cases, a small shelter for the mourners, made of wooden uprights, with wattle or matting stretched between, probably something like the ordinary houses people lived in at the time. All this, the mound, its brick facing and the shelter, were run up in a day, just when required.

Before the beginning of the First Dynasty, this second stage, that of a bricklined pit below and a brickfaced mound above, had been arrived at. The pit was dug in the gravel and roofed with wood. In large and rich tombs the quantity of offerings demanded always more and more space and both pit and mound tended to be much enlarged; but if this process went too far, the wooden roof was found not to be strong enough to cover the wide space and carry the weight of gravel or rubble with which the *mastaba* above was filled. This

GROUND LEVEL

1 — PRIMITIVE PIT AND MOUND

2 — BRICK-FACED MOUND

3 — ENLARGED PIT. BRICK MASTABA ABOVE

4 — BRICK MASTABA — UNDERGROUND CHAMBERS SLOPING STAIR

5 — STONE MASTABA — SHAFT TO BURIAL PIT

1 — GROUND PLAN LARGE IST DYNASTY MASTABA

2 — GROUND PLAN IIND DYNASTY BRICK MASTABA

3 — GROUND PLAN. IVTH DYNASTY STONE MASTABA, GIZA.

GROUND LEVEL

1 — STEP PYRAMID OF SAKKARA.

2 — PYRAMID OF MEDUM.

3 — GREAT PYRAMID.

DEVELOPMENT OF THE TOMB.

difficulty was overcome in the smaller tombs by making a corbel vaulted brick roof instead of a wooden one, while the large tombs were divided up by cross walls of brick, thus forming a row of underground chambers (stage 3), which were all filled with offerings. Tombs of this type (*e.g.*, some of the royal tombs at Abydos, large First-Dynasty tombs at Sakkara, Nagada, and other places) are of considerable size, and the superstructure is built in an elaborate pattern of recesses, probably continuing the tradition of the old structure of wooden uprights with hangings of variegated matting (Ground Plan 1 in diagram).

As wealth increased in Egypt and more and more people wanted to have fine tombs and also to see them finished while they were alive, the constructional difficulties of these large erections became insuperable, if only for the reason that it was impossible to finish the *mastaba* until after the burial had taken place. So the next step was to make a slope or stairway, descending from the ground out on the north side, to the burial chambers, by which the chips from their excavation could be cleared, the coffin could be drawn down when the time came, and the whole tomb, above and below, completed beforehand, so that when the occupant died, nothing remained but to lay the body in place, block up the doorway of his burial chamber with a big stone and fill the descending passage with sand (stage 4).

The superstructure was much simplified at a very early period. The recessed form was given up, and the *mastaba* of the Second and Third Dynasties was a perfectly plain brick building, except for two niches on the east side, which look like the doors of a house (Ground Plan 2). The funeral service was held before the southernmost of these niches and offering jars are often found in place, resting against the brick recess.

By this time metal tools had come into use, and it was much easier in consequence to make the underground part of the tomb larger and deeper. These subterranean rooms are hollowed out deep down in the rock, sometimes they are large and numerous, and seem to reproduce the features of the houses of the living.

Important changes in belief were coming about during the Second Dynasty and a curious stage seems to have been reached at this time when, apparently, the dead man's spirit was supposed to range about freely in his underground abode, but could not leave it to come up above. In the Memphis cemetery, that is to say at Sakkara, on a high ridge above the village of Abusir, there stand rows of brick tombs of all sizes which have recently been excavated, and their arrangement strongly emphasises the idea that at this time the dead man's actual dwelling-place was supposed to be below ground. In the rich tombs there are sometimes as many as twenty or thirty rooms hewn out of the rock, and there is a certain regularity in the plan of them, for the few bones of the dead owners which were found had always been laid in one of the innermost chambers, not directly accessible from the central corridor—an arrangement which we should quite expect for the position of the bedroom in an ordinary house. (Such, indeed, is the plan in the houses of Tell el Amarna, one of the rare sites in Egypt where the dwellings of the living can be explored.) The bones lay on a low, brick-built platform, representing the bedstead, and, curiously enough, an adjoining room was arranged as a lavatory. In most of the other rooms large quantities of stone dishes were found, and there can be no doubt that these were the dishes intended for use at meals, for the food supply of the dead man must have been the principal preoccupation at this time as we know it was later.

The wealthy tombs were so much robbed in ancient times that in some ways more information may be gained from little graves that were too poor to be worth the notice of plunderers. The servants or retainers of the great man were buried down a short shaft or steep stair, at the foot of which was a tiny chamber only about four feet long, which contained the coffin. In this diminutive wooden coffin the body lay buried in the old way of the prehistoric graves, with knees drawn up nearly to the face. But here, it is highly probable that we find the beginnings of mummification, for linen wrappings were often found round the arms and legs and a linen roll lay as a pillow below the head. Cairo Museum possesses two or three of these little coffins—the oldest in the world—and the linen found in them is as good and finely woven as any in later times.

The introduction of metal brought about a new facility in the working of stone, and the indications of the great change in construction that was soon to take place are first to be seen, as we should naturally expect, in the royal tombs at Abydos. The earliest example of anything like a stone building is in the tomb of Khasekhemui of the Second Dynasty, whose burial chamber is lined with limestone. In other of the royal tombs, too, rough stone slabs were found, inscribed with the name of the king or one of his servants who were buried in the adjoining chambers. The first appearance of stone outside the tomb, in private graves, is that a slab with the name of the deceased and a list of offerings was put up above the southern niche. This is a very important thing to be noticed, as it is the first example of the stela, which for thousands of years was the essential part of every tomb; whatever else was there, there had to be a stela.

The stela of Rahotep, from the British Museum, reproduced on p. 24, although dating from the beginning of the Fourth Dynasty, is still somewhat archaic in character and gives a good idea of an early stela. It represents Rahotep sitting at his meal somewhere within the tomb, and the list of food that was supplied to him is written before him and below the table, while the space ruled off in small compartments offers him a menu, or rather a *carte du jour,* showing all the food, drink, linen, perfumes, and other requisites that were placed at his disposal. The large lines of hieroglyphs give some of his titles and his name several times repeated. But the tall objects standing up on the table are impossible to

identify.   Perhaps the most likely explanation is that
they were meant for loaves of bread, laid on the table,
but drawn standing up in a row.

They are constantly met with in still more conventionalised form on Old Empire stelæ and even appear in
much later tomb decoration.

These stelæ, set up outside the tomb, are evidence of
a more advanced idea as to the survival after death, for

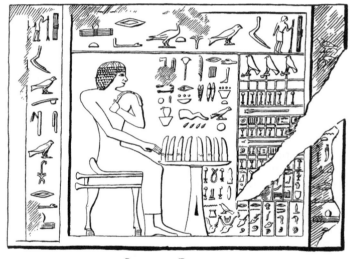

STELA OF RAHOTEP.

now the " Ka " of the occupant of the tomb was believed
to be able to come up, to pass through the false door
formed by the southern niche of the *mastaba* and to
partake of the offerings which were laid in front of it.

Another novelty was introduced about this time, that
of making portrait statues of the dead owner, to the end
that, if anything should happen to the body when the
" Ka " was out on its quest of food, there should be
something similar to which the spirit could return and
find a home.   In early times these statues were shut up
in a chamber, built in the thickness of the *mastaba,* known

as *serdab,* and were never made accessible to the living, but this was a little modified in course of time.

A glance at the diagram (Ground Plan 3) will show that a new feature began to be added to the very simple *mastaba* of the Second Dynasty. Probably the funeral service was becoming more important and more often repeated, and the need was felt of a better shelter for the worshippers than the very temporary tent or wattle structure could afford. The southern niche, or false door, where the stela was, was considered to be the place where the deceased came forth to find his sustenance, and accordingly a small chapel was built on to the outside of the niche, and the niche was opened, a chamber was constructed in the thickness of the *mastaba,* and the niche was transferred to the inner wall of this internal chapel (Ground Plan 3). The next step was that, instead of a little stone slab inserted above the false door, the whole door was made of stone and covered with inscriptions for the benefit of the deceased; that his burial should be under the protection of Anubis, the god of the desert and of cemeteries, and that Osiris should provide sufficient nourishment for the " Ka " for ever. The entire door was henceforward called the stela.

Now, therefore, instead of the main importance of the tomb lying in the underground chambers and their contents, the centre of interest had gradually been transferred to the *mastaba* above, which was provided with a chapel for services, a stela giving lists of the offerings, and a concealed *serdab* for the statues.

This was the state of things about the beginning of the Third Dynasty, but during its short and brilliant course a far greater change took place, one which marks, indeed, an immense step forward in the human progress; no less than the introduction of stone building instead of brick. This tremendous innovation was the work of King Zoser, and here we also come to a parting of the ways in regard to tomb construction, for henceforward kings and ordinary mortals were no longer to be buried in the same fashion. Not only was the royal tomb to be larger and

richer; it was to be different in form from the grave of
any subject. King Zoser changed the type as well as
the place of the royal tombs, for he removed from the old
royal cemetery of Abydos and built on á new plan in the
cemetery of Memphis. His grave, the Step Pyramid of
Sakkara, the oldest stone building in the world, stood at
first alone upon the highest ground of the desert plateau
and looked over the streets and lanes of the archaic
mastabas to the north. But Zoser's building did not
break with the old traditions of tomb construction; it
continued them on a larger scale, for, probably, the
alteration of the superstructure from a flat *mastaba* to a
towering pyramid was not in his mind when he built the
first step. For, see the plan (pyramid 1 in the diagram).
The descending slope from the north, the oblong building, the underground chambers are all those of the old
mastabas, only carried out in stone instead of brick.
How the great idea came to add another and another
stone terrace can only be imagined, but what an extraordinarily magnificent idea it was and how sublimely his
pyramid rises from the featureless western desert !

From this time onwards for some 1,500 years, all the
kings were buried in pyramids, and the subsequent stages
in the architecture are not very difficult to follow.   A
later stage (2) is to be seen in the pyramid of Medum, the
tomb of Seneferu, the first king of the Fourth Dynasty,
where the lower steps have been filled in, though at too
steep an angle, but the highest terrace stands up like a
platform at the top. The finest pyramids, those of Giza
(3), were certainly planned as pyramids from the outset,
though whether they were originally intended to be of
their actual size is open to doubt. How they were built,
how the huge stones were raised into place has been a
matter of amazement since the time of Herodotus, and
the problem is by no means yet solved. Recent research
has found that much was done by means of inclined
planes of brick which were built up against the pyramid
wall and that probably some simple machinery such as
Herodotus has endeavoured to describe, was used for

rocking the casing blocks into place, but in the case of the larger pyramids it is impossible to believe that brick inclines of sufficient size could have been employed, and we are left to speculate and to wonder how, not more than 200 years after stone had first been in use at all as building material, such colossal works could have been accomplished, and accomplished with such extraordinary accuracy. The funeral services for the king were also provided for on a sumptuous scale, for the two parts of the tomb—the burial place and the offering place—were as essential to him as to the private citizen. The stela of the king was set up on the eastern face of the pyramid, and a temple was built outside it where it was hoped and intended that the services for the " Ka " of the deified king would go on perpetually with all the magnificence he had provided for during his lifetime.

The temple was approached by a causeway leading up from the edge of the desert, and the causeway was terminated at its lower end by another temple, or rather a splendid gateway to the precincts. This causeway was one of the first things to be built when the pyramid was begun, as the finer stones which were used in the construction had to be brought by boat in the inundation season and were then hauled up on rollers. When the building was finished, the causeway was roofed over and employed as the entrance for priests and worshippers. The well-known " granite temple " at Giza, often erroneously called the Temple of the Sphinx, is really the valley or gateway temple of the second pyramid, and is much the finest example of such a building; but the whole plan of temple, causeway, and gateway temple, though quite clearly to be seen at Giza, has been most fully worked out by the excavations at the small group of pyramids at Abusir, which were conducted by the Deutsche Orient Gesellschaft (see illustration, p. 35).

To return to the private tombs. These continued to be flat superstructures, stone rather rapidly replacing brick as building material, but reproducing all the features of the brick *mastabas* we have described. Only the underground part was much altered. The centre of interest having now shifted to the chapel above ground, there was no longer any need for the numerous chambers below : the dead man was no longer dependent on that gloomy dwelling, but it was of supreme importance that his body should be buried deep and secure from robbery. With the increased depth of the burial chambers, the sloping passage had become too long for convenience and was abandoned in favour of a shaft, which was sunk through the rock below the *mastaba,* was cased with stone and a small chamber hollowed out at the foot, in which the large stone sarcophagus was placed ready for the burial. The *mastaba* above was then completed, except for the gaping shaft, down which, when the time came, the dead owner was lowered in a wooden coffin ; this was closed up inside the massive stone one, the chamber door was blocked, the shaft filled in with rubble, and covered over like the rest of the *mastaba* roof.

The best examples of this type of tomb (stage 5 in diagram) are at Giza, in the cemetery behind the Great Pyramid. They are all of stone, and all have the two niches on the western side, a *serdab* for the statues, and a chapel.

At first sight we are struck by the number of small shafts surrounding the large tombs ; these are the graves of the great man's servants or dependents, and are to be seen also at Sakkara and other early cemeteries. Dr. Reisner's researches have shown that there was a good deal of reconstruction going on even in the Fourth Dynasty, but the consideration of these points is too technical to be of general interest. The main developments were that the oblong *mastaba* became much shorter in form after the burial shaft took the place of the long descending stairway, and that the internal chapel began to have decoration on the walls in addition to the inscribed stela. At first this was strictly utilitarian and was solely intended as a magic provision for the perpetual renewal of the funeral repast. The pictures of fat oxen, geese, game, legs of beef, vegetables, jars of beer, wine, and milk are extremely well drawn, but there was not much aimed at beyond the abundant food supply. Theoretically, indeed, this applies to all the tomb decoration, for a drink of milk implies a cow, and fish and game have to be caught and trapped before they are eaten, but how much more entertaining to give the artist a free hand to draw all this out on the walls and show the whole scene of the cow being milked, while her calf was held tightly away from her; the herds being driven home through the pools left by the flood where crocodiles were lying in wait and the herdsman chanted a charm against them; hippos being hunted in the marshes with harpoons, the birds snared in a net, fish caught and salted, and crops sown and harvested. So the variety of scenes grew until there is hardly a process of daily life that does not find its place in the tomb reliefs. We can quite well imagine how the owner must have enjoyed going out to the cemetery in the desert on a holiday to see what a beautiful time he was going to have in the next world, and to plan some fascinating addition to his well-filled days. For he is always represented as looking on or taking part in all the work and amusements. He listens to music as he sits at dinner, he rests under a booth out in the fields while the reaping is going on, he is rowed out in a reed boat to catch fish or to boomerang the birds that fly about the marshes; always his figure, drawn in large size, indicates the beginning of a fresh set of scenes, just as a capital letter in modern writing shows the beginning of a new sentence.

These tombs are to be seen in their full development at Sakkara, in the Fifth and Sixth Dynasty *mastabas*, and they afford a picture of life in the ancient world which is unique, both in general interest and in artistic excellence. But it is not absolutely necessary to visit Sakkara in order to get an idea of these decorated chapels, for several of them have been exported from Egypt and set up in European and American museums, and thus many people who will never have the chance to take the journey to Egypt can see the very scenes sculptured and painted by Egyptian artists 5,000 years ago for the great noblemen of Memphis. The stones of the chapels were removed block by block from the *mastaba* to which they belonged and put together again with painstaking care in some far-off land. Such chapels are to be seen in London, Paris, Leyden, Copenhagen, and in Chicago, Boston, Philadelphia, and New York, where the Metropolitan Museum authorities have built up not only the decorated chapel but the entire façade of the tomb of Perneb, thereby greatly enhancing its impressiveness. In this way even the school children of great modern capitals may gain something more than a superficial idea of the daily life, the religion, and the magnificent art of the Fifth Dynasty (Plate II.).

Of course, by the time these chapels were made, the development of the *mastaba* had gone some steps farther, extra rooms and corridors had been added to the original offering chapel, and the decoration had become very elaborate, but the first step was taken back in the brick *mastabas* of the Third Dynasty, when the southern niche was opened and a little offering chamber was made. After that the development is regular, the chapel increased in size, the decorations increased in variety, more and more chapels were added, till we find in the Sakkara tombs that the *mastabas* were really large family burying places, where not only the owner, but also his wife and children have their burial shafts, their stelæ, and their decorated chapels. So, naturally, their plans are much more complex than in earlier times, some chambers and corridors were added on at later periods, and the building as a whole is often irregular in shape. The largest tomb of all, that of Mera or Mereruka, a nobleman of the court of Teta, a king who reigned towards the end of the Sixth Dynasty, contains over thirty rooms, mostly covered with reliefs and probably reproducing the features of a great house of the time. While the superstructure thus grew always larger and more imposing, the small burial chamber underground remained for a long time perfectly plain and undecorated. It is only during the present year—1922—that renewed research has found that the latest of the large Sixth-Dynasty tombs had inscribed burial vaults.

All these changes in custom are certainly the outcome of a development in religious beliefs. The conception of a life after death which prevailed in the Old Empire may have been very material, but at all events it was a most constant preoccupation and we cannot rest satisfied without trying in some measure to understand what the underlying ideas were. In origin they were surely simple enough. The spiritual part of the man, that part of his personality that went on, is known in Egyptian as the " Ka," and is written with two upstretched arms.

Much paper and ink have been spent in the effort to explain what the " Ka " may have been, but the Egyptians certainly never defined their views for the benefit of posterity, and the ancient ideas of it varied and developed to such a degree that nothing but confusion seems to result from search of this kind and it may be more profitable to turn away from Egyptian sources altogether. For Egyptian thought in primitive times must have been very much like the thoughts of other primitive peoples, and it would be a great help to our understanding it if it could be shown that some similar ideas are widely held by other races in regard to the continuance of life after death.

That this method of approaching the subject has something to recommend it may be seen in the following quotation from the first page of Macdougall's " Body and Mind," a work of entirely philosophical aim, taking no account of ancient Egypt or of any special people, yet giving an extraordinarily good description of what the " Ka " must have been :

" The belief most widely current among peoples of lower culture is that each man consists, not only of the body which is constantly present among his fellows, but also of a shadowy, vapour-like duplicate of the body ; this shadow-like image, the animating principle of the living organism, is thought to be capable of leaving the body, of transporting itself rapidly, if not instantaneously, from place to place . . . and of manifesting in those places all or most of the powers that it exerts in the body during working life. Sleep is regarded as due to its temporary withdrawal from the body . . . death is thought to imply its final departure to some distant place."

Macdougall also quotes to much the same purpose from Tyler, " Primitive Culture," Third Edition, Vol. I., p. 424.

Here is then, evidently, the same idea so far spread among primitive people as apparently to be the most natural way of thinking. The originality of the Egyptians did not lie in their having evolved the idea that the principle of life in an organism is a separate entity, a shadowy, vapour-like duplicate of the body, but in the extraordinary logical process by which they followed it up. So long as the body existed, the " shadowy duplicate "—the " Ka "—would have its own accustomed abode to inhabit, and so the body must be kept free from disturbance and its tissues rendered as indestructible as possible : hence the process of mummification and the precautions against robbery. The " Ka " was the animating principle, which could not die so long as it was sustained and nourished; hence the provision of offerings, the tomb decoration, the portrait statues, the priests dedicated to its service, and the endless invocations reiterated down the centuries. It is typical of the Egyptian reverence for the past that this very primitive idea should have gone on, mingling with lofty and noble moral principles and rules of conduct, and that the crude old belief persisted, not merely as a ritual observance, but apparently as a reality, as long as the Egyptian religion lasted. No doubt this extreme conservatism is responsible for much of the appalling confusion presented by most Egyptian myths; the early story was simple and barbaric, later versions were added but the first were not discarded; so, in the case of Osiris and other universally worshipped deities, the contradictions and contrasts in the tales are past reconciling, for, so far, these stories have only come down to us in very late form. But if late Egyptian thought, in all its mingled crudity and subtlety, remains still, for the most part, a closed book to us, it is something, at least, that we can see that its beginnings were as the beginnings of other peoples and that the mystery which envelops those early searchings after truth is no other than the great mystery which is common to all humanity.

3

CHAPTER III

OLD EMPIRE

(3000–2500 B.C.)

PART I.—FOURTH DYNASTY

FOR all the foregoing it has been necessary to go carefully into little bits of evidence, pore over museum cases, piece together records of excavations and compare them with the scanty remains of archaic Egypt, but with the coming of the Fourth Dynasty this is entirely changed. Its mighty monuments are standing for all to see, and by far the best way to understand the Old Empire is to go again and again to Giza and Sakkara and take time to realise what is there. For not only are the massive structures and huge blocks that we have learned to expect to be found there, but also an exactness in measurement and a delicacy of execution which bespeak a love of accuracy for its own sake that was never again attained to in Egypt and has rarely been surpassed anywhere.

A description of the Pyramids cannot be entered on here; our purpose is rather to try to reconstruct in thought the cemeteries as they once used to be; to look, at Giza, for the group of pyramid, temple, causeway, and gateway temple; to see the processions of worshippers arriving at the lower entrance, parting to go in by the doors of north and south, meeting within to do obeisance to the royal statues, then sweeping on up the causeway to the temple itself, where white-robed priests recite strange, long hymns and lay offerings of food and drink and flowers for the dead king before his altar.

The diagram on p. 35, showing a restoration of part of the pyramid plateau, is helpful, though perhaps not quite certain in all particulars. The second pyramid group is

34

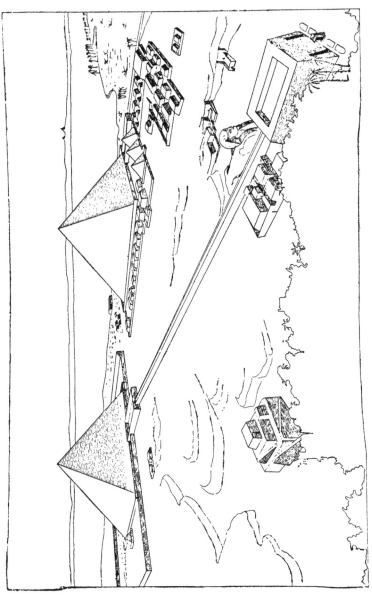

First and Second Pyramids and Sphinx after Hölscher's Reconstruction.

complete, with the enclosure wall, the temple on the east side, the long covered causeway, and the granite temple at the foot. Near the Great Pyramid are rows of *mastaba* tombs of the noblemen of the Courts of Cheops and Chephren, and outside the temple on the east are three little pyramids, supposed to have belonged to the daughters of Cheops. In the foreground is a small unfinished pyramid, interesting only because it shows the brick ramps used in the construction. When visiting the Pyramids we should certainly try to see some of the private graves of the nobles, for these have been so little used in subsequent periods that it is becoming possible, thanks to excavations, to get a good impression of what the cemetery looked like nearly five thousand years ago. The long lines of streets and cross streets behind the Great Pyramid are so regular that it seems certain that they were planned by the builder of the pyramid, and this is fully borne out by research, for, though there is plenty of variety in the structure of individual tombs, they all belong to the Fourth-Dynasty type (diagram of tomb development, p. 20). That is to say, they had begun to have decorated chapels, *serdabs* for the " Ka " statues, and deep shafts sunk to the burial chamber.

Plate III. is a splendid granite sarcophagus from the Cairo Museum. As a rule these large Old Empire coffins are quite plain, but the finely cut pattern of this one recalls to us the recessed *mastabas* of the First Dynasty.

It is the coffin of Khufu-ankh, who was probably a son of Khufu, or Cheops, the builder of the Great Pyramid, and it was found in a chamber at the foot of one of the deep shafts behind the pyramid.

Similar to the Giza *mastabas,* but a generation earlier, are the tombs of Medum, which surround the Pyramid of Seneferu, the first king of the Fourth Dynasty (see diagram of tomb development, p. 20). Some of the most beautiful works of ancient art come from these tombs, the most famous being the statues of Rahotep and Nefert and a painting of geese, all in the Cairo Museum. The British Museum has a very fine stela from the tomb of

Rahotep (p. 24), extremely delicate in execution. The title on the statue of Rahotep is "Commander of troops," and it is most likely that Seneferu sent him on expeditions against the Beduin ; at least, the traditional scene of the king grasping his enemies by the hair is inscribed upon several large blocks of sandstone which have been brought from the quarries in Sinai to the Cairo Museum. It is also known that he sent ships to Syria for cedar wood, and the traffic up and down the Nile with granite from Assuan and alabaster from Middle Egypt must have been constant. Seneferu and his successor Cheops, or Khufu, began to write the royal name in a new way. Hitherto it had been inscribed on what looks like a banner, but was more likely meant to represent the palace door (*cf*. Hieraconpolis Palette, p. 12). After the beginning of the Fourth Dynasty it was enclosed in an oval ring, known as a cartouche, and, though the old sign did not disappear from the royal titulary, it was not much used except in formal proclamations.

Khufu's great pyramid, with the statues and sarcophagi of the period, mark the zenith of the Old Empire art, which in exactness of proportion and finish of execution attained then a level that was never again reached. The only portrait of him, unfortunately, which the Cairo Museum possesses is in striking contrast to the size and splendour of his grave, for not a vestige of all the statues which must once have adorned his temple remains, and his features are only preserved to us by a tiny ivory statuette, found at Abydos. There are, however, numerous portraits of the two following kings, the builders of the second and third pyramids. The magnificent basalt statue of Khephren (Khafra) in the Old Empire room in Cairo originally stood at the end of the central aisle of the granite temple near the Great Sphinx. This was the valley, or gateway temple of the second pyramid, and, in its austere splendour, is one of the grandest monuments of Egypt. Its only decoration was a series of twenty-three statues of the king, the places of which are easily to be distinguished on the temple floor.

These statues, at some time unknown, were thrown into a shaft, probably a grave of later age, which was sunk through the floor and from which the great statue and fragments of eight or nine others were recovered.

Dr. Reisner has excavated a large part of the Giza cemetery, including the valley temple of the third pyramid, that of Mycerinus or Menkaura, where he found several statues of the king and some interesting groups, sculptured in green slate, which formed part of the temple decoration. The portraits of the king are extremely fine in technique, but, taken on the human side, his features are coarser and less dignified than those of Khephren's splendid statue. Perhaps the finest of them is in Boston Museum, but Cairo possesses two or three large alabaster figures in fair preservation, as well as three of the groups in green slate, where the king stands between the goddess Hathor, patroness of Upper Egypt, and the local divinity belonging to a province. The existing groups are all of provinces of Upper Egypt, but originally there was probably a complete set of the nomes or provinces of the north as well as the south. This temple building is a great contrast to the magnificent granite temple, for Mycerinus died before either the pyramid temple or the valley temple were completed, and his successor finished them on a much cheaper scale than was first intended. In the pyramid temple one or two blocks of fine basalt, with which the walls were to have been lined, are set up in place, but it is evident in many parts that the rough walls were merely plastered over and painted to look like basalt or granite. We should hardly have expected the Old Empire artists to have been capable of this, but it is, unfortunately, not very uncommon. The valley temple was built of brick and offered nothing of interest beyond the statues; it was accordingly filled in again.

Thanks to these excavations, Boston has also acquired a large number of the " Ka " statues from private tombs. These portraits of private individuals were, as has been said, made for the tomb and not intended to be seen by

visitors, but for a magical purpose, to the end that the
"Ka" might be provided with a body which it could
inhabit in the event of anything happening to the
mummy.

Cairo has a superb collection of these statues, nearly
all found in *serdabs* of tombs at Giza and Sakkara, and
most other museums have at least one or two specimens,
one of the most deservedly famous being the figure of a
squatting scribe in the Louvre. These statues vary
enormously in merit. The best of them, Rahotep and
Nefert, the Sheikh el Beled, the charming little female
figure presumed to be that of his wife (Plate IV. 1) the
Louvre scribe, and a few others, are works of art of a
very high order indeed; many more are good and delicate
carvings, but some are frankly bad and look as cheap as
no doubt they were.

The figure is almost invariably portrayed as being in
the prime of life and of a vigorous build, the chief exception to this being the portrait of a little dwarf, whose
misshapen body is rather mercilessly rendered. It is
quite intelligible that the "Ka" should want the cor-
poreal form it might be obliged to inhabit to be a likeness of what it was at its best, but it is doubtful whether
the statue of the dwarf was made so characteristic because
the "Ka" could scarcely have been comfortable in an
ordinary figure, or whether it was so made by order of
some great man, who may have owned the dwarf as a
pet and plaything in this life and wanted to keep him on.
These statues are, it is needless to say, by far the oldest
in the world, they are of unique interest, and the finest of
them have the quality of all great art, that the more our
knowledge of them grows, the more our admiration of
them deepens.

PART II.—FIFTH DYNASTY

When we pass to the next dynasty a considerable change appears to have taken place in the country, and the worship of Ra has become so prominent that it is generally believed that the priests of Ra of Heliopolis must have ascended the throne. A story is in existence entitled "How the kings of the Fifth Dynasty came into the world," which embodies an old tradition that the wife of a high priest of Ra bore to the god three children at a birth, who became in course of time the three first kings of this dynasty.

In any case, from this time onwards the kings professed themselves to be the bodily sons of the sun-god, and they incorporated the name of Ra with their own names and titles. This is an important point to keep hold of, for the solemn fiction of the physical descent from the god was carefully kept up and exercised much influence on Egyptian history down to late times.

Unhappily nothing remains of the great temple of Ra at Heliopolis, but one of his shrines, built in the Fifth Dynasty, is within easy reach of Cairo at Abu Ghurab, near Abusir, about two-thirds of the way from Giza to Sakkara. It was very possibly built on the model of the Heliopolis temple, and is the oldest temple to the gods, the oldest purely religious edifice, as distinguished from the funerary temples of the deified kings, which Egypt, or indeed the world, possesses.

This sanctuary consists of a mound, once the base of an obelisk, with an enclosure wall and a large open courtyard, where stands a huge altar of alabaster. On the desert side, west of this, is a brick-built, boat-shaped erection, which represented the Barque of the Sun at his festival. The obelisk, the oldest of which there is any mention, was shorter and thicker than those of later date, but standing, as it did, high on its base, it must have formed a landmark visible across the valley from Heliopolis, and its metal cap may have been designed to catch the first beam of morning light from the rays of the god as he rose on the eastern horizon and to flash them back to the mother shrine.

The funerary temples of three of the Fifth-Dynasty kings are very interesting indeed, and their preservation so good that it has cleared up the whole subject of pyramid architecture. They are all at Abusir, and so much remains of their plan that they are much easier to understand than the temples of the Giza Pyramids. Some idea may even be formed of their original magnificence, for the basalt floor, the broken granite columns, and the fine slabs of limestone from roof and walls, are still impressive even in their ruin. New York Museum shows a complete model. Many of the best of the sculptures are in Germany, but the Cairo Museum has some splendid granite pillars and a very fine set of reliefs in the west gallery. The inadequate lighting makes it difficult to do justice to the delicacy of execution which characterises these sculptures, but they are of unvarying excellence and of considerable interest historically. One large fragment shows the goddess Eileithuia, patroness of childbirth, suckling the king; this is almost certainly a piece from a scene referring to the divine descent of the king, how he was begotten by Ra, fashioned by Khnum, and reared by the other gods, and it is by much the earliest example of the kind. The illustration on p. 42 shows part of the detail of a large scene representing gods bringing in foreign captives. The gods are in an upper register, each one holding the rope by which the captive below is bound. It is of great interest to try to identify the foreign nations or races with whom Egypt was fighting at this very early period. In our illustration, Nos. 1 and 4 are Libyans, No. 2 a man of Punt (? southern Arabia), No. 3 an Asiatic. It is difficult to give an idea in a small reproduction of the fine and subtle line of this scene, which is characteristic of good Old Empire sculpture, but even on this small scale the different types of features are well brought out.

Not every visitor has time or is sufficiently interested

in the subject to make a special trip to the Abusir temples, though the excursion is much to be recommended, but practically everyone does see at least once the tombs at Sakkara, and from the glorious picture-book unrolled on the walls of Ti and Ptahhotep, more is to be learned about the Fifth Dynasty than could be told in many chapters. And it is the same to some degree with everyone who knows any of the fine decorated tomb chapels

FOREIGN CAPTIVES.

that have been transported to museums : they will see there the very scenes sculptured in the Old Empire, sometimes still brilliant with colour, sometimes left unfinished after the owner's death. Once familiar with these complete chambers we shall recognise many separate blocks of relief which have found their way to museums, some, perhaps, torn from their place in the tomb and sold by robbers, some found detached from their surroundings—stolen, it may be, but a short time after they were set up. These have greatly less meaning than when seen in place in the tomb chamber, but they are often very beautiful in workmanship, such as those shown in Plates V. and VI. Both of these are in Cairo Museum and are fine examples. Plate V. shows the owner of the tomb sitting at the table enjoying his meal. The upper part of his large figure is broken away, and we can only see his feet and legs and a few of the food offerings which are heaped up in front of him, but in the row below him is the orchestra, for the Egyptians liked music with their dinner, and here we have, first, two singers clapping their hands to keep time, then a harpist, a flutist, and lastly a player on a long reed pipe. Below these are dancing girls doing a step-dance and two more singers.

Plate VI. has a good deal of colour still and is in beautiful low relief. It represents a favourite scene of fighting boatmen and gives opportunity for a very free treatment of the human figure as well as the introduction of plants and other accessories. The papyrus boat is bright green, the figures are red, and traces of blue remain on the water and on the lotus flowers. A famous example of this scene is in the tomb of Ptahhotep, but time fails for even the shortest description of these wonderful figured walls.

In these private graves the burial chamber is un-decorated, the coffin generally rather plain, and all the labour and expense is lavished on the chapel above ground. The essential part of the decoration is not, however, the pictures, but the stela, or false door, before which the offerings were laid. On it are inscriptions in vertical lines, always in much the same words, praying Osiris that when the voice should go forth—*i.e.*, when the funeral ritual was recited, there should appear on the table of offerings meat, game, and all sorts of good and pure things. Here Osiris appears as the provider for the continuance of life, while on the other side of the stela the prayer is to Anpu or Anubis, figured as a jackal, the god of the desert and of cemeteries, whose function it was to watch over the dead, that the burial should be undisturbed. On entering the Museum of Cairo and turning to the left, we pass between two lines of such coffins and stelæ, all of which come from rich tombs at Giza and Sakkara. In the south-west corner are large stelæ with the table of offerings in place before them.

A picture of the funeral service is often shown in the tombs. As each dish is laid on the table by a kneeling priest a libation or liquid offering is poured by another priest standing behind; others bring food and rolls of linen, while the " chief reader " repeats, from a papyrus he holds in his hand, the prescribed formulæ which accompany each offering. Sometimes, as in the tomb of Ptahhotep, there is a little entrance room with a shelf, on which the dishes were placed while waiting their turn; in another case, in the tomb of Ka-gem-na, there is a large stone block beside the altar, which evidently must have been intended for a sideboard.

There is also at Sakkara a royal tomb, the pyramid of Unas, belonging to the end of this dynasty, which is easy of access and is worth seeing, as it is inscribed inside with what are known as the " pyramid texts." These were composed long before King Unas' time, are, indeed, believed to date from before the union of the north and south and certainly are the most ancient religious documents in the world. They partly consist of early myths handed down by the priests of Ra of Heliopolis, but mostly refer to ceremonies for the deifi-cation of the king and the ritual connected with his subsequent worship. As they are in the funeral chamber, where no living being was ever to enter, these texts must have been for the use of the dead king alone, that he might know what awaited him among the gods, how he might fly as a bird, cross the heaven in the boat of Ra his father, or feed with the gods on the never-ending offerings of his subjects on earth. The offerings were brought to his temple on the east side of the pyramid, where, as we have learned from the temples of Abusir, the decoration referred not only to the supply of food and other bodily wants in the next world, but also to the exploits of the king while he was on earth, and was intended to be seen by all the worshippers in the temple. The language of the pyramid texts is very difficult, the forms are extremely archaic, and the thoughts often crudely primitive, but the meaning is being gradually arrived at as knowledge of the language advances, and their importance is generally recognised as being the basis for most of the Egyptian mythology of later times.

PART III.—SIXTH DYNASTY

This long dynasty, the last of what is known as the Old Empire, closes with the fall of Memphis and the break-up of the royal power, but its earlier part shows no decline from the preceding centuries; rather, indeed, an extension of the authority of Egypt under a vigorous line of kings. Somewhat more definite history of this period has been preserved than has been the case for the previous dynasties, for the custom of recording personal matters in a man's tomb had begun, and there are one or two very precious bits of biography which throw some light on the extent of the empire and the duties of courtiers and viceroys.

There is in Cairo an inscription from the tomb of one Una, a nobleman in the reign of Pepi I., which tells how he was sent to command an army against the eastern Beduin. This was considered a specially important expedition and from the wording it would seem that he crossed the desert and pushed through part of southern Palestine. He also went south against the Nubians and cut a canal round the First Cataract to facilitate the passage of the boats. From this time onwards, whenever Egypt was wealthy and prosperous, there was always the question of the Sudan trade and the necessity of guarding the Egyptian frontier and the trade routes. Lower Nubia—the district between Assuan and Wady Halfa—is so very barren a region that it can never have produced much that Egypt wanted; yet Egypt always had to keep hold of it because of the steady demand for gold and other things from the Sudan, and even from central Africa, which were brought down the Nile by negro traders. The general name for all countries south of Egypt is Nubia or Ethiopia, which is "Kush" in the early books of the Bible and "Kash" on the Egyptian monuments.

Pepi I. went himself to Assuan and there received the submission of the chiefs of Lower Nubia, and it is quite in accordance with his great interest in the south that he should have made gifts to the ancient temple at Nekhen or Hieraconpolis in the old southern capital. We have seen in the preceding chapter that the treasure buried there did not consist exclusively of objects of the archaic period, but that there were also two important pieces a thousand years later in date. Both of these are in Cairo Museum. One of them is a life-size statue of Pepi I. in beaten copper, with a little figure of his son, afterwards king, beside him; the other is the golden head of a hawk which almost certainly was a new idol dedicated by Pepi in the temple. When these things were discovered some years ago, the Pepi statue was found broken and cast away indiscriminately among a mass of older objects, but the sacred figure of the god had been treated with much more reverence and had been placed carefully resting on a tall rod overlaid with copper, which stood inside a stand of pottery, and the whole was enclosed in a small cell beneath the temple. Perhaps it may have been removed from its place in the temple for fear of plunderers, or it may have been ceremonially buried at some later time and a still more splendid image may have replaced it in the shrine above.

The technique of all the copper work is the same: the metal is not cast but beaten into plates and hammered on to a wooden core which had entirely disappeared. Unfortunately the plates covering the body of the hawk were very thin and so completely corroded that when the air reached the fragile film of rusted metal it collapsed into fragments, but the superb golden head, in perfect condition, is to be seen in the jewel room. Happily, enough remained of the inscription which covered the base of the large statue to put the identification beyond doubt. It is, of course, by far the oldest life-size metal statue in existence.

Plate IV. 2 shows the smaller statue, that of Mehti-em-sa-f, who succeeded his father as King of Egypt. It was badly broken when found and has been well mended and set up, only the upper and lower halves of the figure must originally have been separated by a wooden frame-work overlaid with electrum or gold leaf, forming the garment, which was a sort of kilt, the ordinary Old Empire dress. There was certainly also a jewelled head ornament. The eyes are made in the usual way, the iris of rock crystal with a flake of ebony behind it which gives a lifelike sparkle, while the white eyeball is modelled in ivory.

Another light on the extent of Egyptian dominions to the south comes from the " Grenfell " tombs at Assuan, where a noble family lived who seem to have been hereditary governors of the southern province and entitled " judges attached to Nekhen and caravan con-ductors for the King." Their duties were to collect tribute and secure the trade routes from the southern Sudan, and, as one of them, Herkhuf by name, was a very bold and adventurous person, he made no less than four journeys to a distant country called " Yam " and brought from there a tremendous booty—incense, ivory, ebony, boomerangs, skins of panthers, slaves, and, best of all, a little dwarf to dance for the king. King Pepi II., who was then a boy, was so delighted to hear of the coming of the dwarf that he wrote a letter to Herkhuf with his own hand, bidding him make haste, for that His Majesty looked forward more to seeing the dwarf than to all the treasures of the Land of Punt, but above all things to take the greatest care of him on the way and to have ten people sleeping beside him at night on the boat to make sure that he did not fall overboard. Herkhuf was so much honoured by this letter from the king and by all the good things that followed on it that he inscribed the whole correspondence, along with the accounts of his Nubian journey, on his tomb wall at Assuan.

Besides these southern princes there were several powerful hereditary chieftains in other parts of the country, at Sheikh Said, Dendera, and other places, and it is noticeable that, even at Sakkara, the tombs of the noblemen are extremely large and costly, while the pyramids of the kings show a decided falling off; still, there seems no question at all of the supreme authority of the king throughout this dynasty.

It is still to Sakkara that we turn for most of what is known of the daily life of the time, and the tombs of Mereruka and the rest of the group which surround the pyramid of Teta contain an even greater variety of scenes than those of Ti and Ptahhotep, though the artistic quality of the work is not quite so fine. Still, the scenes of hunting in the papyrus marshes are admirably rendered, the drawing of birds and animals is as good as it could well be, with perhaps a little less restraint, a little more freedom from convention—for instance, in the hippopotamus hunt in the tomb of Mera, or the snaring of birds in that of Ka-gem-na—than has yet been noticed.

During this dynasty a new feature in burial customs should be observed which points to a real development in belief. In place of the portrait statues which were in general use during the earlier centuries there now appear little figures of servants occupied in all sorts of domestic work. The meaning of this must be that the " Ka " no longer was supposed to require an additional material body to give it security, but that it was possessed of greater freedom of movement and permanence of duration, and that its requirements could be attended to in the next world; in short, that it not only needed a food supply, but servants to prepare it. Cairo possesses a good number of these statues of servants in painted limestone, and the Haskell Museum at Chicago has lately secured a good set, but they are fairly rare, and, though not nearly so fine artistically as the old " Ka " statues, are of considerable importance as foreshadowing a great change in the burial customs. Here, and also in the appearance of the coffins about the end of the Sixth Dynasty, we can see the beginnings of what is usually known as the " Middle Empire " type of burial, and if this fact is taken in conjunction with the political state of the country, where the rise of the powerful provincial nobility foreshadows the coming feudal state which is found fully established by the Eleventh Dynasty, it will be seen to afford strong evidence that the obscure period which intervened between the fall of Memphis at the end of the Sixth Dynasty and the rise of the Middle Empire cannot have been very long.

CHAPTER IV

THE FIRST DARK AGES: DYNASTIES VII.-XI.
(ABOUT 2500-2000 B.C.)

WHAT the catastrophe may have been which overtook Egypt at the end of the Sixth Dynasty is quite unknown, but it was most complete. Probably there was foreign invasion as well as internal disturbances; in any case, the tendency already noticed of a weakening of the royal power and an increase of independence among the nobles culminated in a break-up of the monarchy and a period of total confusion.

The next light that is shed on Egypt shows the country, two or three centuries later, divided among local chieftains, more like what it had been in prehistoric times than the centralised state it had for so long become. There is no certainty as to how long these dark ages lasted, and most various estimates of their duration have been given, ranging from less than three centuries to more than fifteen. The dating of the Old Empire and all its monuments hangs on this, and it is naturally a matter of great importance for all the history.

There is a date for the *end* of the period, as there is good evidence that the Eleventh Dynasty began about 2160 B.C., but it is not known how long the gap was between the end of Dynasty VI. and the beginning of Dynasty XI. Archæological evidence, however, is clearly in favour of the time having been short, and although a great many names of kings who reigned during these centuries are recorded, in such an epoch of turmoil and confusion kings probably followed each other in rapid succession, or may even have reigned at one and the same time in different parts of Egypt. The likelihood is that the shortest possible dating, as given above, is not very far wrong, but it is to be hoped that future excavations will enable the question to be satisfactorily answered. It should be said, too, that the dating given here for the Eleventh Dynasty and the Middle Empire, though considered to be correct by most scholars, is not universally accepted. The dates given, for instance, in Professor Flinders Petrie's history and in the British Museum catalogues will be seen to give a higher antiquity to this period.

That the names of kings were handed down to later times at all shows, however, that it was recognised that there was a reigning house, or rather reigning dynasties, whose titles were acknowledged throughout these disturbed centuries, but their authority must have been confined to a comparatively small district. Instead of there being a large metropolis for the whole of Egypt where all the greatest people lived, died, and were buried, there were only scattered towns ruled by local chiefs, which gradually grew in wealth as the country recovered from its disasters; so in this way rich and important tombs of this period may be found in any part of the country. But " rich " is used in a relative sense only. The days of beautiful sculptures and gorgeous temples were over for a time. No expeditions went to Assuan or Sinai to fetch fine stones; if such were used at all they were torn from the temples and tombs of a more prosperous age. The kings of Dynasties VII.-X. probably lived at Heracleopolis in Middle Egypt; other great families were settled near that part of the country as well as farther south, and the old cemetery at Sakkara was still in constant use, for Memphis must have been a large and important city, although it had lost its place as the capital. But there are no great monuments of this period, and its archæology must be worked out from more or less insignificant tombs, while any knowledge of its history has to be gathered from records of the state of the country before and after it. The conditions of Egypt under the Old Empire and Egypt as it emerges again in the Eleventh and Twelfth Dynasties are very different indeed. In the first it is a despotic monarchy, in the second a feudal state.

So long as the country was unsettled or devastated by invasion the nobles had only the modest revenues of impoverished estates on which to live and hold their little courts, and the kings probably only differed from the others by having an acknowledged divine right to the throne, but as things settled down and the wonderfully fertile soil was again cultivated in a regular and systematic manner, wealth increased rapidly and allegiance to the monarch came to consist not only of tribute but of military service, for the boundaries of Egypt always required protection against the Beduin of the desert and the Sudanese on the south. Changes, religious as well as political, came about, for a good many alterations in burial customs were introduced during these centuries, and all of them point to a more widespread sense of a personal survival. We have seen how strong the belief in some form of immortality was from the earliest times in the case of kings and great men, but, as far as we can judge, at that distant date it was only those who could afford themselves *mastabas* and statues that could have much hope of realising it, for the tombs of the poor were very bare, and if the soul had indeed a journey to take into the other world he had very small provision to take along with him.

But during the dark ages there grew up a custom which made it much more possible for a man of moderate means to go into the future life with a good equipment and, incidentally, to give the chance of survival along with him to a number of his dependents. We have seen how, even before the end of the Sixth Dynasty, little stone figures of servants were beginning to take the place of the old " Ka " statues.

This idea gained ground, and as time went on the figures were made of wood, quite cheaply, and more of them put into the grave, so that there came to be not merely single figures of servants, but whole groups and scenes. These are mostly taken from domestic life;

granaries with little compartments for the different kinds
of grain, houses with open courtyards where oxen are
being killed and dressed and dough prepared for the
making of bread and beer, but besides these there are
sometimes carpenters' and potters' workshops, other
scenes connected with the occupations of the deceased,
and very frequently boats, some rigged for sailing up-
stream, some for rowing down.

These things are seldom artistically made; the wood
is generally of poor quality and the painting crude, but
they are extremely entertaining, and to work through a
good set of them gives a delight such as an inventive
child must feel over a new kind of mechanical toy. The
little doors that open and shut, the toy portmanteau
which the great man takes with him on his *dahabieh*, the
cabin where he sits in state while the crew work hard
and the *reis* calls out his orders from the prow, the box
of wood and copper tools from the carpenter's shop, give
us a touch of fellow-feeling for the people who were at
such pains to make them, which perhaps we have not
been able to feel when looking at their greater works.
And the best of these models are really charming. Two
companies of soldiers, one Egyptian and one Sudanese,
have been well known for a long time, and are among
the most popular objects in Cairo Museum. In the
spring of 1920 American excavators, working for the
Metropolitan Museum, found a splendid set of models
in a tomb high up among the limestone precipices of the
Theban Hills. The tomb had been robbed in ancient
times and explored recently, but the New York diggers
detected a few bricks closing up a cavity in the rock wall,
and through a chink between two bricks could just descry
the gleam of colour. When the bricks were removed an
astonishing array of brightly painted figures met their
eyes. So absolutely dry and free from dust was that rock
crevice that the finger-marks, wet with plaster, of the
workman who put the things in place, were plain upon
one of the boats. When laying the bricks to close the
cavity this boat had stuck a little too far out, and the
Eleventh-Dynasty mason gave it a push with his wet hand.

All these figures look as if they had just left the workshop where they were made. The modelling is very good and many of the scenes are novel. Besides the usual boats, granaries, and household scenes, there are remarkable representations of a garden with a copper tank in the middle, surrounded with trees, the house at one end and a high wall round about. These are unique; also a large scene of cattle inspection, while the weaving and carpentry, though not the first examples found, have many new points of interest. The models have been divided between the Metropolitan Museum and Cairo, and, by the kindness of the New York authorities, I am enabled to publish illustrations of two of the finest, the scene of cattle inspection and one of weaving, as well as a rowing-boat (Plates VII. and VIII., A and B).

Plate VII. shows the cattle being driven into the presence of the owner, who sits under a raised and covered portico, with several clerks beside him provided with writing materials to take the accounts. Before him, on the ground, the foreman bows respectfully and presents the list. The cattle, of several different breeds, are marched past by the herdsmen.

The scene of the loom (Plate VIII.A) is much the best in existence, and gives a good deal of information about the processes of spinning and weaving. The three sitting girls and the three standing in the middle are spinning and winding, two are setting out the yarn on the wall, and the remaining two are working at the loom. The preservation is marvellous, for even the original linen thread is still fairly strong, and the whole process has much resemblance with Beduin weaving at the present day.

In Plate IX. another scene is figured. It was not among the Theban models, but was found some years ago at Sakkara, and is of a rather earlier date. The peculiarity here consists in its being frankly a scene of amusement, with no sign of any useful household occupation or any preparation for dinner. The master of the house sits in his (portable) arm-chair, two harpists squat beside him, three singers clap their hands in time to the music, while a woman sits at his side to enjoy the entertainment with him.

In the style of the coffins, too, inside as well as outside, great alterations took place during these dark ages, the beginnings of which were discernible before the end of the Old Empire, and the full development of which is present in the Twelfth Dynasty. It was felt that the dead man needed something more to help him against the dangers of the unknown, and that, moreover, he would be the better to have along with him the means of providing for his more obvious wants. That this could be done by the help of magic, which would give reality to written words or painted objects, was fully believed, so inside the coffin pictures were painted of food, jewellery, clothes, flowers, and such other things as were wanted in everyday life, and in addition there began to be religious texts as well, magic formulæ for the use of the spirit in the other world; and it is significant of the change in beliefs that the earliest of these inscriptions in coffins are practically identical with parts of the pyramid texts which had been intended in old times for the king alone. An untouched burial of this period is a most solemn and impressive sight for anyone who has the good fortune to see it. The body is carefully mummified and wrapped in abundance of linen sheets and bandages; the head, covered with a brightly painted mask, rests on a wooden or alabaster pillow, and is turned sideways to look through a painted false door and to read with greater convenience the magical inscriptions which run round the coffin. Outside the door are painted two eyes, which really represent the dead man looking out on the world, though all these sacred eyes have a double symbolic meaning, connected with the eye of Horus, which, as having been offered to his father Osiris as the magical food which should effect his resurrection, became a sort of religious name for the food offering. Fine sets of these very interesting coffins may be studied both in Cairo and in the British Museum. In both collections they are arranged in chronological order, so far as space permits.

The more valuable of these coffins are enclosed in an

outer case of coarser wood on which the two eyes are repeated. In the burial chamber, outside the coffin, besides the equipment of model figures, there is always a set of four vases, known as Canopic jars, in which the internal organs were placed after their removal from the body. These are found at least as early as the Fifth Dynasty, but at first they were very plain stone jars with flat lids, whereas by the time now under discussion the lids were generally human-headed, and later it was usual to have them all four different—one human, one jackal, one monkey, and one bird. They form one of the regular pieces of tomb furniture from this time onwards. These sets of jars were kept in boxes known as Canopic chests; many of them are in all museums.

As the history of Egypt emerges from the chaotic condition of the dark ages, several of the noble families are found to have attained to something like royal state, but it is not until the Eleventh Dynasty that there is a really strong royal house. Up to that time the acknowledged kings of the country had lived at Heracleopolis in Middle Egypt, but the Eleventh Dynasty came from much farther south, and were, in fact, the hereditary princes of Erment and Thebes, which now, for the first time, appears as a prominent city, and under a succession of strong princes took its place as the principal town of Egypt. But although these princes were recognised as the Eleventh Dynasty of Egyptian kings, the feudal conditions were maintained under them, and the hereditary nobles at Beni Hassan and other provincial towns had absolute authority over their vast estates and kept up a court almost equal to that of the king.

The Eleventh-Dynasty kings were mostly called Antef and Mentuhotep; they were all buried at Thebes, but their pyramids must have been small and insignificant, except, indeed, that of Mentuhotep III., who made a new departure in the type of the royal burying-place, and, instead of being buried in his pyramid, hollowed out a deep tunnel in the cliffs of Der el Bahri for his tomb chamber, and built a little pyramid in his funerary temple outside of it.

Part of the causeway leading from the edge of the desert to this temple has lately been uncovered, and we can still see in the ground the roots of the trees that Mentuhotep planted to border it, and an open space in front of the temple, where trees were planted in a grove, which must have looked extremely beautiful as a foreground to the white colonnades surrounding the pyramid and the great cliffs which rise behind. But all the water for the trees had to be brought over a considerable stretch of intervening desert. One wonders how long the funds for such a purpose lasted out. These groves gave the model to Hatshepsut, who centuries after brought incense-trees from Punt to make beautiful the garden of her father Amen Ra at Karnak and the road that led to it from her own temple at Der el Bahri.

The Eleventh-Dynasty temple is of quite a novel kind and aroused much surprise when it was uncovered a few years ago. It stands to the south of the larger temple of Queen Hatshepsut, built long afterwards in the same magnificent surroundings, and for which it served as a model in many ways. The little pyramid in the centre of Mentuhotep's temple was an entire change from the old idea of the pyramid as the royal burying-place, and the innovation was probably followed by some of his successors, though this is only known from pictures. Behind the temple and supplementary to the king's burial were the tombs of five women, each of whom styled herself " the only royal favourite." The coffins of two of these ladies of Mentuhotep's *harîm* are now in Cairo, and are the most important objects belonging to this period from the artistic point of view. There is a certain hardness, one might say a touch of the archaic, about them, which is natural when we think how long it was since the flourishing days of the Old Empire and how Art had to rise again out of the ruins. On one beautiful limestone coffin, besides the usual representation of the door with two eyes and the necessary outfit of offerings, we have a detailed description of the lady having a drink of milk, in the form of a story told in pictures. First, the cow comes along with the calf, then the cow is hobbled to be milked and sheds a tear of grief that the nourishment she gives is being taken away from her offspring, then the milk, in a lordly dish, is taken to the lady, who drinks it while she is having her hair done. Another very interesting piece from this dynasty is a fragment of bas-relief, where we see the figure of King Antef IV. with his hunting dogs, all named. The British Museum has some good reliefs from the temple of Mentuhotep, discovered by the Egypt Exploration Fund Expedition.

By the end of the Eleventh Dynasty we reach the Middle Empire, one of the most brilliant periods of all the history of Egypt, and also we come at last to solid ground in the matter of chronology, for here astronomy comes to our help. The fragment of a letter exists from a priest, dated in the 120th year of the Twelfth Dynasty, notifying his subordinates that the feast of the rising of Sirius would take place on the fifteenth day of the eighth month. That is to say, there was then a discrepancy of 225 days between the first of Thoth, which was held as New Year's Day, and the day of the appearance of Sirius above the horizon at sunrise, which was the "ideal" New Year's Day by the calendar; this date is fixed by astronomy as 1880 B.C., so that the beginning of the Twelfth Dynasty can be safely put at 2000 B.C., and is the earliest Egyptian date about which there is any certainty.

Here, too, we may note a nearly contemporary date on which Assyrian scholars seem to be agreed—that of Hammurabi, the great Babylonian king and lawgiver, who is generally identified with Amraphel, King of Shinar, one of the kings mentioned in Genesis xiv.

Hammurabi is believed to have reigned about 2100 B.C., and as, by the account in the Old Testament, Abraham took part with the King of Sodom against him, we have fairly good ground for believing that the journey of Abraham from Ur of the Chaldees into Palestine must have happened some time during the Eleventh Dynasty of Egypt.

CHAPTER V

MIDDLE EMPIRE: TWELFTH DYNASTY

(2000-1788 B.C.)

THE Middle Empire was one of the greatest ages of Egyptian history. Its kings carried the arms of Egypt across the desert, over the hills and valleys of Syria to the shores of the Euphrates; they ruled the Sudan as an Egyptian province, traded round the Eastern Mediterranean, planned and executed immense works of irrigation, and built or restored almost every temple in the country. Moreover, all of the work of this period which has been preserved is of a very high quality indeed, especially remarkable for delicacy of finish; but we are not in so good a case in regard to the large buildings as to those of either the Old or the New Empire. Nothing of the Twelfth Dynasty remains so outstanding as the Pyramids of Karnak, for in the Middle Empire the pyramids were small and poor, while the pyramid temples, which were magnificent, have been totally plundered. The one great monument of theirs which we can go to see from Cairo is the obelisk which Sesostris (Usertesen III.) erected before the temple of his father Ra at Heliopolis. It is the oldest known obelisk of the tall, slender form, as distinguished from the shorter and thicker one built at Abu Ghurab in the Fifth Dynasty (p. 40), and there were originally two of them; the other is said to have been destroyed in the thirteenth century A.D.

As was seen in the last chapter, Egypt had climbed out of the chaos and confusion of the " dark ages " and had become once more a powerful state, but this time it was rather on the lines of a feudal monarchy than of an autocratic empire, for it was divided into provinces, each of which was governed by a family of hereditary nobles owing allegiance to a more or less powerful sovereign.

In the Eleventh Dynasty some of the Antefs and Mentuhoteps had evidently been able to exert a real authority over the whole country, and with the advent of the very vigorous line of Twelfth-Dynasty kings Egypt was once more thoroughly consolidated by means of military expeditions and large public works, but the feudal form of government remained and the local nobles still lived like little kings, each with a retinue of guards and a staff of officials. Probably this is the reason why no real capital city and no great cemetery is specially associated with this period, but large and important tombs are to be found in many parts of Egypt.

The earlier of the kings were buried in pyramids not far from the old Memphis cemetery, at Dahshur and Lisht, for, though Theban in origin, they did not consider Thebes convenient as the seat of government. The first king of the dynasty, Amenemhat I., moved northwards, and he and his son Sesostris I. built their pyramids at a place now known as Lisht, where they still may be seen from the railway near the little station of Matania, about midway between Bedrashein and Wasta. Recent excavations have shown that the temples of these pyramids were very large and splendid; that of Sesostris I., in part cular, was surrounded by a massive wall built in a niched and recessed pattern and decorated with fine reliefs. From this temple come the nine portrait statues of him in the Middle Empire room at Cairo, and the figures of Osiris, also portraits of the king, which stood in niches on either side of the entrance corridor. The technique of the statues is rather stiff and mechanical; they do not seem to have been coloured, and perhaps they were not quite finished when put in place.

The two small brick pyramids at Dahshur belong to two later kings of this dynasty, Amenemhat II. and Sesostris III. They are somewhat different in construction from the Old Empire type, for although the entrance is on the north side as before, the opening to it is placed on the ground some distance outside the pyramid, and a long passage leads down to the funeral chamber. All were, of course, robbed in antiquity, but by a fortunate slip on the part of ancient thieves one or two well-concealed boxes of jewellery have been found in recent times hidden in these passages. These jewels are among the greatest treasures of the ancient world and are quite marvellous in design and execution. If we take the Khephren statue, the Sheikh el Beled, or Rahotep and Nefert as the highest point reached by Old Empire art,

PECTORAL OF USERTESEN III.

what will live in our minds as the most beautiful works of the Middle Empire are some of the necklaces and pectorals from Dahshur. The illustration shows one of these. The king's name is enclosed in the cartouche in the middle, protected by the outstretched wings of the vulture, the emblem of Ra. On either side, the king, symbolised as a lion with the head of an eagle, tramples on the prostrate bodies of his negro and Asiatic enemies. The materials used in the pectoral are lapis-lazuli, carnelian, turquoise (or blue glaze), and very fine gold cloisonné. All the jewellery from the Dahshur find is in the jewel room of Cairo Museum, but an important set of objects—also royal jewellery—of this period was found more recently at Illahun by Professor Flinders

Petrie and has been acquired by the Metropolitan Museum. We should note here, also, that among the jewels are some very fine scarabs and scarab seals, which begin to make their appearance at this period. Scarabs were used in many ways, the most common being simply as a seal, for which purpose they were engraved with the name of the owner. Everyone carried a scarab seal, and used it not only to sign documents, but to stamp the dab of clay which was the ordinary fastening over the knot of string which tied on the lid of a box or jar. Besides these personal or " private " scarabs, they were much used as amulets, the beetle, from having the meaning of the verb to " become " or to be " transformed " being connected with the idea of a future life. Scarabs were also used to send greetings and wishes for a " Happy New Year " from one friend to another, and occasionally they were specially made to commemorate great events or to be placed in foundation deposits below the corner-. stone of a temple or pylon. Another kind, known as a " heart scarab," is more suitably noticed later. The British Museum possesses what is probably the finest collection of scarabs of all kinds and periods in existence.

The novel designs in the gold filigree jewellery of this period ought not to be passed without mention, as they undoubtedly show a foreign influence; and, as there is known to have been much traffic with Crete at this time, these gold objects were probably brought to Egypt from there, wherever their actual place of origin may have been.

Other Cretan remains have been found near the pyramid of Sesostris II. at Illahun, where that king built a town and may have resided, but the place was abandoned shortly after his death, and the things found there may be pretty securely dated to his reign. Mycenæan scholars assign the painted pottery fragments found there to the " Middle Minoan " period of Crete.

This choice of Illahun as a site marks the beginning of the great activity of the Twelfth Dynasty in connection with the Fayum, for it was by their energy and resource

that this fertile oasis became a part of Egypt. Traditions
of this colossal work were still current in the time of
Herodotus, who speaks of the Lake Moeris as being
artificial and having been made by a king of that name,
but since the language has been better understood it has
become clear that the name was merely a corruption of
the throne name of Amenemhat III., who completed the
work of reclamation of the Fayum which had been begun
by his predecessors. In the earliest times, before there
was a regulated irrigation system in the Nile Valley, the
Fayum was a great lake surrounded by marshes, into
which not only the Nile water found its way at high
flood, but the drainage water from the low lands near the
western desert escaped by means of a channel now known
as the Bahr Yusuf. There was an outflow to the Nile
near Beni Suef, by which the water returned to the Nile
when the river had fallen sufficiently low to receive it.
The levels have been carefully verified by engineers of
the present Irrigation Department, and the achievements
of the Middle Empire have really only become clear since
the physical conditions were correctly understood.

The scheme of the Twelfth-Dynasty Irrigation Department was to build a dam across part of the lake so as to
hold up the water to a certain height and to place regu-
lators on the channels of in and out flow, by which
means the lake would act as a reservoir where the flood
water could be stored during high Nile and let out again
when the Nile was low, thereby assisting the agriculture
and navigation in the Delta, as well as adding a large
tract of fertile land reclaimed from the marshes. A town
soon rose on this new ground, on the site of the present
Medinet el Fayum, and must have been a pleasant place,
with a view over the lake and fresh breezes from the
water as well as good air from the surrounding desert.
Amenemhat III. probably made it his capital; in any case,
he chose the shore of the lake for his burying-place, and
built his pyramid at Hawara, near the sluices he had
made to control the waters. And he made a pyramid
temple so great that it should be a place of worship for

all Egypt to pay him honour and to behold his mighty works for all time. For it is accepted by most scholars that the famous Labyrinth, one of the wonders of the world, described by Herodotus, who saw it, as surpassing even the pyramids, was no other than the funerary temple of Amenemhat III. Herodotus tells of the twelve courts, six facing north, six south, its vast halls and corridors all of fine white stone and full of sculptured figures. Alas ! its beauty was its undoing, for now, although the pyramid adjoining it is still marked by the rubble core which rises like a little mound, a tract of sand furrowed by trenches and strewn with countless chips of stone is all that remains of this most beautiful of temples.

There is an interesting statue of Amenemhat III. in the museum, in hard quartzite, and some other portraits of him, which show curious features with very marked cheek-bones. This peculiarity has given rise to all sorts of speculations on his descent and his descendants and to comparisons with the so-called " Hyksos " statues (p. 75), but such conjectures have nothing to support them except some physical resemblance.

The kings of this dynasty succeeded each other as Amenemhat and " Usertesen," as the name used to be written, but it is now recognised that it is more correctly rendered as Senwsret, which was transliterated by Greek writers as Sesostris, and it is the name of the Pharaoh Sesostris III. that has passed into classical legend as one of the great conquerors of the ancient world. He profited by the wealth of a well-governed country to make great military expeditions, far into Asia on the one hand, and Libya on the other, but these were rather in the nature of successful raids than permanent settlements, whereas in the Sudan Egyptian supremacy became so complete that the lower part of Nubia up to the Second Cataract was treated as an Egyptian province, and recent explorations have brought out the fact there was an Egyptian governor in the Twelfth Dynasty even as far up as the modern Dongola, who was buried there with much state and surrounded by a retinue of servants who had been sacrificed to bear him company. Fortresses were built at Semneh, Kummeh, and other strategic points, and all the way down the river careful observations were made of the levels reached by the water at the inundation time.

It is probable that another very important piece of engineering was undertaken during this dynasty, no less a work than the cutting of a canal to connect the Nile with the Red Sea. Such a canal certainly existed in later times and was ascribed by the Greeks to Sesostris. It was taken off from the Nile near where Cairo now stands and passed north of the Gebel Ahmar, down the Wadi Tumilat to the Bitter Lakes.

Throughout all this dynasty Egypt flourished exceedingly. It must not be forgotten that in several parts of the country the local noblemen were almost like lesser kings; they had prospered with the prosperity of the land, and their tombs are among the most splendid in Egypt. At Beni Hassan, El Bersheh, Meir, and other places there are chambers cut in the rock and decorated with paintings which were once as beautiful as we should expect from a generation whose craftsmen could make the Dahshur jewellery, but it is heart-breaking to see the fragments from which we have to reconstruct the glory that has gone.

In the Beni Hassan tombs, which are the most complete, the preservation is so bad that it is doubtful if the ordinary visitor with half an hour to spend ever sees anything more than dull-brown walls with indistinguishable streaks of paint over them and here and there traces of a large figure. Yet not a century ago these tombs must have been as gorgeous with colour and covered with pictures of daily life as interesting and in much greater variety than those in the tombs at Sakkara. Their decay was hastened by the proceedings of the first discoverers, who, in their eagerness to see and copy quickly the scenes that they considered the most important, rubbed the whole surface over with varnish, which may have heightened the colour for the time, but made it far more difficult for their successors to decipher any of it,

5

especially as these paintings are not in relief, like Sakkara, but flat on a plaster backing. The drawing of a hoopoe in an acacia (" saunt ") tree will give some idea of the wealth of detail with which these scenes abound. Anyone going to see Beni Hassan is much recommended to look beforehand at the publication of the tombs by the Egypt Exploration Fund, which is very full and careful.

Among the scenes there is a very famous one representing some Asiatics—the Aamu—coming up to offer

HOOPOE.

tribute. The Semitic type of face, the dress and embroideries are most carefully drawn and are extremely interesting. It has been suggested that the picture represents the arrival in Egypt of the Children of Israel, but there is no foundation for this, for traffic was evidently constant between Syria and Egypt at this time, and it may quite as well have been any other incoming families of Asiatics or Beduin from Arabia; but undoubtedly the scene gains in interest from the fact that it must have been about this time or not much later that the migration of Jacob and his descendants did take place.

The poorer people meanwhile were still being buried with sets of little models such as had come into use during the " dark ages " between the Sixth and Eleventh Dynasties, but these went gradually out of use. Some rather coarse-looking coffins in Cairo Museum, with granaries and boats on the top, came from Beni Hassan, from the slope below the cliff from which the big tombs overlook so grand a view of the dead owner's estates. We notice the coffins still have the eyes outside and long lines of inscriptions and painted objects within. Religious ideas were developing, and these long texts had come to be needed by every man as a protection against the dangers that were to confront him in the next world. It appears, too, that character was going to count in the next life and not solely the abundance of things that a man possessed. Ameny, one of the nobles buried at Beni Hassan, says in his tomb among other virtuous actions, that he had never oppressed the poor, that he had never used unpaid labour, that there was none hungry in his province in his time. The Metropolitan Museum is particularly well furnished with objects of this period, thanks to their excavations at Lisht, round the pyramids of Amenemhat I. and Sesostris I. An unplundered private tomb, belonging to a lady called Senebtisi, now in the Museum, offers a great deal of interest and has been most admirably published. In Cairo and in the British Museum are many good coffins of the period as well as large collections of Canopic vases and other pieces of funerary furniture.

But towards the end of the Middle Empire changes begin to appear in the burial customs. The little figures of servants and domestic scenes are no longer found, and their place is taken by small statuettes in the form of mummies. These were meant to be servants also, but they point to a further development in religious conceptions connected with the worship of Osiris, which came very much to the front during this period. He was the god who had been dead and come to life again, and his cult, which had been hitherto specially concerned with the provision of a food supply for the dead, from now onwards is associated with the growing belief in his function as judge in the underworld. He is depicted as a mummy, being the god of the dead, and probably the provision of servants for the deceased in mummy shape signifies that, in the world of the dead, inmates of that world would be allotted to them for the work to be done there. These figures are called *ushabtiu* or "answerers," but as they properly belong to a later period it is sufficient to note here that they do occur in the Middle Empire, and leave a detailed description of them to a time when they are more usual.

The literature of the Middle Empire was considered classical in later ages, and a certain amount of it has survived, though it is rather curious that out of the few papyri extant some three or four are fragments of the same story. It is the Tale of Sinuhe, or Sanehat, an Egyptian who escaped to Syria and lived there for many years, finally returning to Egypt in his old age. It has some literary merit and a good deal of interest at the present time, as giving the earliest picture of Syria in existence, and showing that the civilisation of Syria at the time of the Middle Empire—about 2000 B.C.—was far behind that of Egypt.

Sinuhe, apparently a prince of the blood royal, took a sudden alarm when King Amenemhat I. died and the news was sent to the Crown Prince, Sesostris I., who was at the time absent on a military expedition against Libya. Whether Sinuhe had any pretensions to the throne himself, or why he should have been in such terror of the new king, the story gives us no idea; in fact, he is at great pains afterwards to assure the Syrian chief with whom he took refuge that he had never done anything wrong, but that a sudden impulse had seized him. "Behold this flight that I made, I did not have it in my heart, it was like the leading of a dream. There was no fear, there was no hastening after me, I did not listen to an evil plot, my name was not heard in the mouth of the magistrate, but my limbs went, my feet wandered,

my heart drew me." But however innocent and loyal
Sinuhe may have been, he seems to have run at his
hardest to get out of Egypt. He crossed the river on a
raft without a rudder somewhere near where Cairo now
is, passed the Gebel Ahmar, hid by day and travelled by
night till he got out beyond the frontier fortress on to the
Arabian desert, where, by-and-by, fatigue and thirst
overcame him and he sank down exhausted. "I dried
up, my throat narrowed, and I said ' this is the taste of
death.' Then I lifted up my heart and gathered strength.
I heard voices and the lowing of cattle; I saw men of the
Sati (a Beduin tribe) and one of them, a friend to Egypt,
knew me. He gave me water and boiled milk for me, I
went with him to his camp." From there he went on
from tribe to tribe till he came to the country of Edom,
and finally was sent for by a prince of the hill country
who had heard of him from some Egyptians at his court.
This prince it was who tried to get out of Sinuhe why he
had left Egypt. Sinuhe assured him that he really did
not know why, but there he was, and the King of Egypt
was a great god and Amu-an-shi and all his people could
not do better than send him their submission, "for he
refuses not to bless the land that obeys him."

The prince does not seem to have adopted that sug-
gestion, but he treated Sinuhe extremely well, gave him
the choicest of his land, and his daughter in marriage.
For many years Sinuhe lived happily in the foreign
country, but as age drew on his heart turned more and
more back to his own land, and at last he sent a petition
to the King of Egypt for his forgiveness (not that he
ever had done anything wrong!) and the permission to
return. To this the King of Egypt sends a gracious
reply which is very characteristic of the Egyptian point
of view. After assuring Sinuhe of his continued affec-
tion and pleasure at the prospect of seeing him, the letter
goes on to say that he will be received as chief among
the companions of the Great House (Pharaoh), and that
as Sinuhe must be now growing old and thinking on the
day of his burial, he was to be assured of a great funeral

with the courtiers following his coffin, which "shall be in a gilded case, the wood painted with blue, a canopy of cypress wood above thee, and oxen shall draw thee, the singers going before thee and they shall dance the funeral dance. Thou shalt not die in a strange land, nor be buried by the Amu; thou shalt not be laid in a sheep-skin when thou art buried; all people shall beat the earth and lament over thy body when thou goest to the tomb."

Sanehat's grateful reply is also given at length, and the tale closes with his joyful return to Egypt, his wel-come in the palace by the king, the queen, and the royal children, who sang an ode in his praise, "waving their wands and sistra," and how afterwards he was taken to his house, "the house of the king's son, in which were delicate things, a place of coolness, fruits of the granary, treasures, clothes from the royal wardrobe, the finest of perfumes in every chamber and all the servants in their places. Years were removed from my limbs, I was shaved and polled my locks of hair, the foulness was cast to the desert with my garments. I clothed me in fine linen and anointed myself with the best oil of Egypt, I laid me on a bed, I gave up the sand to those who lie upon it, the oil of wood to him who would anoint himself therewith." Lastly, he says, "There was built for me a pyramid among the pyra-mids . . . my statue was inlaid with gold, its girdle of pale gold, His Majesty caused it to be made; such is not done to a man of low degree. May I be in favour of the King till the day of my death."

CHAPTER VI

THE SECOND DARK AGES

(1788–1580 B.C.)

THE mysterious period that lies between the Middle and the New Empire is full of puzzles, the answers to some of which, at least, are probably lying deep down under the salt marshes of Tanis in the north-east Delta. It may be that they will never be found; still, anything may happen in Egypt, and scientific digging with ample funds will doubtless some day unearth unlooked for treasures from that reluctant and ungrateful soil—or at any moment a stela or a scrap of papyrus might turn up at Sakkara or elsewhere that would shed light on one or other of the points at issue.

At the end of the Twelfth Dynasty Egypt was very powerful and prosperous; a few years more and it was plunged in disorder, a prey to local strife and foreign invasion. The first two or three kings of the following dynasty—the thirteenth—seem to have ruled over the whole country and probably had their capital in the Fayum, for the kings' name best known to us is Sebek-hotep, so called from Sebek, the crocodile god of that province. But disaster soon overtook them, and Egypt broke up again into petty princedoms all more or less under the sway of an alien race.

Outside of Egypt the veil lifts a little and we get glimpses of the surrounding peoples. Syria was becoming much more civilised, while round about the Mediterranean coasts and the islands commerce had developed extensively, and there were many prosperous and settled communities living a peaceful and ordered life, under the hegemony of Crete. As was noted in the last chapter, there was trade between Crete and Egypt as early as the Twelfth Dynasty, and during the centuries we are now considering the great palaces at Knossos and Palæokastro were built and decorated in the magnificent and extraordinarily modern style which has been the surprise of recent excavations.

Crete must have flourished exceedingly throughout this age, but over Egypt all is darkness. All that is known for certain is that Egypt was conquered and ruled over by foreign kings, who were called the Hyksos by Manetho, an Egyptian priest who wrote the history of Egypt in the time of the first Ptolemies (300 B.C.); that the capital of the Hyksos kings was at Tanis in the Delta, that two or three of these kings were supreme over the whole of Egypt, though during the greater part of the period the south was able to retain practical independence; and lastly, that it was a powerful southern family who took the lead in the expulsion of the invaders.

But we cannot leave this dark period without further comment, for its obscurity covers what is to many people the most interesting part of Egyptian history—the sojourn of the Children of Israel—and this accordingly would seem the most suitable point at which to discuss, or at least to state, the problems of the Oppression and the Exodus. To the obvious question " Who were the Hyksos?" there is no satisfactory answer. The translation given by Josephus, the Jewish historian, of the word Hyksos is " Hyk," a prince, and " sos," a shepherd, and from this they have generally been called the " Shepherd Kings." But this is a most uncertain reading, and it is much more likely that the word in Egyptian really meant " Ruler of Countries," and that the Hyksos kings were lords over a vast empire which embraced northern Egypt along with Syria and part of Asia Minor.

Josephus believed that the Hyksos were the Children of Israel, who were not driven out of Egypt as the Egyptian historian avers, but led out by Moses according to the account in the Book of Exodus, and to prove this he quotes at length from Manetho and combats the accusations of the historian against the invaders. But this testimony of Josephus was entirely discredited by the Egyptian scholars of the last century, and a tradition accepted which, while admitting that the Children of Israel probably came into Egypt under the Hyksos kings, would place the date of the Exodus as late as the reign of Merenptah (1225-1215 B.C.).

A good many scholars, however, guided by some evidence which was not in possession of the older generation of Egyptologists, are inclined to come back to the idea that Josephus knew what he was talking about, and though not suggesting that the Jews were actually the Hyksos kings, they consider it likely that the date of the Exodus is very near that of their final defeat and expulsion.

There is not much in the Bible account to favour one theory rather than the other; we are told that Joseph married the daughter of the High Priest of On (Heliopolis) and that Moses was found by Pharaoh's daughter, but as there was always a high priest at Heliopolis and all the kings were called Pharaoh, there is nothing to be made out of that.

The reasons in favour of the earlier dating are briefly as follows :

1. The silence on the Egyptian side of any mention of the presence or departure of the Children of Israel is easier to understand if the Exodus took place at a time of national upheaval when there was a great movement for the expulsion of foreign tyrants under vigorous kings of Egypt.

2. It has generally been felt by Old Testament scholars that to place the date of the Exodus under Merenptah (1225-1215 B.C.) and the settlement in Palestine even as little as forty or fifty years later, leaves too short a time for the events to have taken place which are chronicled in the Books of Joshua, Judges, and Samuel, down to King David, who cannot have reigned much, if at all, after B.C. 1000.

3. In the Tell el Amarna tablets, which are letters in the Babylonian language, written from Palestine about 1400-1360 B.C., during the reigns of Amenhotep III. and Akhenaten, by Egyptian governors and rulers of semi-independent Syrian states, great complaint is made of the inroads of a certain desert people, called the Khabiri, who were attacking the country from the east and were burning towns, massacring the inhabitants, and settling themselves in the country. The etymology of the name is said by cuneiform scholars to be a fair rendering of the word " Hebrew." Now, if the Exodus did not occur till the later date, this remains an incomprehensible allusion, but if the Children of Israel went out along with, or soon after, the last of the Hyksos, it becomes a very reasonable account of the settlement in Palestine from the point of view of the inhabitants.

4. In a long inscription of Merenptah, chronicling his victories in Libya and in Syria, there occurs the first mention of Israel in the Egyptian language, and he speaks of Israel as one of the settled peoples of Palestine. When this stela was first found this was felt to be rather an awkward fact to have turned up, as it had not previously been much questioned that Merenptah was the Pharaoh of the Exodus, but if the earlier dating be accepted and the Khabiri recognised as the invading tribes of Israel who had been settled in Palestine for a century before the time of Merenptah, it would be a perfectly natural thing that he should put them along with the other peoples of Syria and Palestine in his list of conquests.

Against this view and in favour of the other are the following considerations :

1. If the Exodus took place at the beginning of the Eighteenth Dynasty, and the Children of Israel are to be identified with the Khabiri, the period of the wandering in the wilderness must be lengthened considerably over the " forty years " given in the Old Testament. In reply to this it can only be observed that " forty years " is admittedly used in an arbitrary way in many passages.

2. The names of the treasure cities, Pithom and Rameses, could hardly occur before the Nineteenth Dynasty. This objection is obvious and is the chief difficulty in the way of accepting the earlier dating, but a close examination of the Egyptian proper names, that of Joseph, his father-in-law, and other persons in the story, has brought out the fact that they are distinctly names which belong to the Twenty-sixth Dynasty (633-525 B.C.), and as no one could possibly refer Joseph or any other part of the narrative to so late a date as that, it follows that the form of the names must be due to the editor of the last recension; probably Ezra the scribe, who lived about 460 B.C. and gave the Egyptian names in the form in which he was most familiar with them, regardless of archæological accuracy.

There are difficulties about both theories, and though we may lean to one rather than to the other, it is better to admit that the question can hardly be answered satisfactorily on the facts as they are known at present.

Turning to the monuments, we are confronted by a blank almost more complete than that of the records. Some strange figures of black basalt in Cairo Museum used always to be attributed to the Hyksos, partly because they looked so very different from anything else, but chiefly because they were found at Tanis, and because the oldest of the many cartouches inscribed on them is that of Apophis or Apepi, one of the Hyksos kings. And it used to be said that as the Hyksos were probably Semitic they were not artists, that they left very few sculptures, and that these few did not look Egyptian. But it must be admitted that if these statues do not look Egyptian, still less do they look Semitic. They are extremely fine in their massive ugliness, and there is no doubt about the skill of the sculptors who could hew the tough black rock into such characteristic forms. But it is more likely that they are of a far higher antiquity and that they are solitary survivors of the oldest art and civilisation that flourished in the Delta.

A Hyksos king, who must be mentioned here, however, is Khyan, monuments of whom have been found as widely apart as Crete and Baghdad. If only his features were known it might be possible to gain some idea of what race he belonged to, but by bad luck there only exists one statue of him, and of that only the base. The feet and the name are there, but no more. It is of black basalt, not unlike the Tanis statues, but was found at Bubastis (Zagazig).

A good many scarabs of the Hyksos period are found both in Egypt and in Syria and are pretty easily recognisable.

Very few other objects, large or small, can be assigned to this age. If there was any distinctive art or style about the Hyksos monuments, other than the scarabs, examples of it must be sought for in the Delta, and especially at Tanis, where, perhaps, much information may yet be gained as to the state of Egypt during these centuries of chaotic confusion.

CHAPTER VII

NEW EMPIRE: EARLY EIGHTEENTH DYNASTY

(1580–1411 B.C.)

WE now reach the greatest epoch in the history of Egypt, when, having thrown off the foreign yoke, her own armies under her own kings extended her power over all the neighbouring lands, and, just as we have to go to Giza and Sakkara to get an idea of the splendid art and the free, simple life of the early dynasties, so to realise what Egypt was at her mightiest we must visit Luxor and Thebes.

It is indeed a revelation to see the temples at Karnak and Luxor, still so majestic in their decay, which the kings of the earth built to the glory of their divine father, and those others, hardly less gorgeous, which they reared in the cemetery across the river to their own; and to visit the valley where they are buried and follow the path which their funeral processions once trod, farther and farther into the recesses of the desert cliffs to the cavernous openings of their tombs, then to descend through corridors and halls painted with strange, bright-coloured scenes of gods and men and demons, till, at last, the chamber is reached where the Pharaoh once lay, surely in the grandest resting-place ever devised by man.

Such things are seen by every visitor and will not fail to impress even the most hasty and impatient traveller. but those who have more time to spend will find that the smaller private tombs whīch honeycomb the Sheikh Abd el Gurneh Hill are no less wonderful. They are a mine of wealth for Egyptian scholars and all students of ancient history, for not only do the pictures and bio-graphical notices which they contain give the chief source for what is known of the private life of the Egyptians, but there, and there alone in the world, are pictures of other peoples, Syrians, Negroes, Hittites, Cretans, Phœnicians, bringing their wares and the products of their lands as tribute to Thebes, fifteen centuries before our era.

Although what remains in these tombs to-day is perhaps the hundredth part of what has been lost, it is still to them that we look for light on many sides of Egypt's past; and though to visit them requires time and patience to scramble up and down a hot hill-side and to wait, when we step out of the blinding glare into the half-dark of a little rock-cut chamber, until our eyes can pick out the scenes—often, alas! fragmentary and defaced—yet once we begin to see for ourselves and to find scraps of beautiful painting, graceful figures of dancers, spirited hunting scenes, processions of foreign captives doing obeisance or bringing gifts of gold and ebony, Syrian and Mycenæan vases, the fascination of the place takes hold of us, and we look back on days so spent as some of our best memories of the best place in Egypt.

Unless Thebes has been visited, the fine collections of Eighteenth-Dynasty art in Cairo and other museums lose a great part of their interest, but most museums are rich in objects from Thebes, and it is well to become as familiar with them as possible so as to understand better the changes in custom and religion that have come about.

The architecture and decoration of the tombs in the New Empire were on a very regular model and follow in essentials the arrangements of the earlier times, in that the outer part is mainly concerned with the daily and the public life of the owner, while the stela and the food supply, on which his continued existence depended, occupy the inner and more private chambers. As the Theban tombs are not *mastabas,* like those at Sakkara, but are hollowed out of the rock, they are more uniform in plan and consist usually of a forecourt and a **T**-shaped internal chamber, the cross part of which is fairly well lighted and contains the scenes of daily life with the titles and occupations of the deceased, while the long limb of the **T** running back into the cliff shows the funeral procession carrying the tomb furniture, groups of sorrowing relatives and professional mourners following, and at the far end a shrine where statues of the dead man and his wife generally stood. In theory the burial shaft would be found below this inner part, but this is not often actually the case, and it may be under any part of the tomb or outside it altogether. There frequently are several shafts belonging to one chapel. The burial chamber at the foot of the shaft, where the coffin was placed, was undecorated, but a good deal of furniture was put into it, and these objects had changed considerably since the Middle Empire.

Ideas of immortality had evidently extended very much, for people of ordinary and small means now felt that they could expect their wants in the next world to be attended to, but that their welfare there depended greatly on their conduct in this one and also on the precautions which they were able to take to ensure the protection of the gods in the future state. The magical texts and mythology connected with the passage of the dead through the underworld to the Judgment Hall of Osiris, and the trial to be conducted there, had by this time grown to such dimensions that they could no longer be written on the coffin, but required a long roll of papyrus to contain them. This collection of magic texts is called the Book of the Dead, and was placed inside the coffin on the mummy.

The model statuettes of servants which were such a marked feature of the graves of the early Middle Empire have entirely disappeared, and their place is taken by numbers of little mummy-shaped statuettes, the presence of which was noted at the end of Dynasty XII. That these also were servants intended for the use of the dead is evident, not only from the inscriptions they bear, but also from the hoes painted on their shoulders and the bags for tools on their backs. Rich fields were the Egyptian idea of Paradise, and their *Champs Elysées* were understood most literally; but rich fields have to be tilled, and a man did not want to spend his time in the next world ploughing and sowing, so these little figures were put into the tomb to do the drudgery for him. These are among the most familiar of all Egyptian antiquities, owing to the vast numbers of them which exist as well as their rather attractive appearance; they are often made of good glaze and of a beautiful colour. They are known as *ushabtiu* or "answerers," because their function was that, when the name of the deceased master was called on to perform the tasks which fell to him to accomplish, they should be there to answer for him. In the Eighteenth Dynasty they are not nearly so numerous as they afterwards became, but as they are a regular accompaniment of every burial this seems the most suitable place to notice them.

The types of the coffins have also changed considerably from the old style with eyes on the outside, which were so well known in the Middle Empire. There is from the Eighteenth Dynasty onwards a great deal more variety about them, far too much indeed to enter on any description here, but the large collections in Cairo and in the British Museum may be studied chronologically.

After the collapse of the Middle Empire under foreign invasion, some of the chief southern families appear to have been able to retain a measure of independence and even to have ranked as kings, who must have been contemporary with the much more powerful Hyksos monarchy in the north. On the plateau above Drah Abu'l Neggah, on the west bank of the Nile opposite Luxor, there stood once several little pyramids which belonged to kings of the Fourteenth Dynasty. They were called Antef, like their forerunners in the Eleventh, but practically nothing is known about them, for the history of Upper as well as of Lower Egypt is most obscure during the centuries of Hyksos rule. It may, however, be assumed that the south was never completely under the Hyksos yoke, and about 1600 B.C. we find a powerful Theban family taking the lead in the long struggle for emancipation, which ended in the expulsion of the invaders. These Theban chiefs were reckoned as the Seventeenth Dynasty, and three of them in succession were called Sekenenra. The mummy of the last of them has the skull cleft by the blow of a battle-axe, so it is fair to suppose that he was killed in battle in the hard fighting against the Hyksos, and by some writers the dynasty is considered to close with his death.

Something must now be said on the peculiarities of the Egyptian succession laws, so far as they are understood, and the guiding principle for us to lay hold of is the old theory of the physical descent which we have noted as early as the Fifth Dynasty (p. 40).

In old times the king was called the son of Ra; in the Middle and New Empires, when Ra had become identified with Amen the Theban god, the king is accounted the son of Amen Ra, and the belief was that at some time the god had become the father, by a mortal mother, of the ancestor of the dynasty. Thus, though it was almost unheard of for a woman to reign, the succession had to go on in the female line.

Once this fiction of the divine descent was accepted, we can easily understand that the marriages of brother and sister became almost a necessity in order to keep the divine blood uncontaminated. So long as a son born of two divinely descended parents succeeded his father the dynasty would have an unchallenged right, but when there was no son, or when the throne was usurped, the successor seems invariably to have legitimised himself by marrying a princess of the old royal family, in whose veins the divine essence was still supposed to flow. Later on in this dynasty, when there was any doubt about the claim of the reigning sovereign, we shall see that the old myth was enacted over again, and an actual interposition of Amen Ra himself was declared to have occurred.

Fuller records exist about the Eighteenth Dynasty than about any other period, but the beginnings of it are somewhat obscure, and scholars are not in agreement as to who was the first king. It is quite clear, however, that the title to the throne was transmitted by an heiress, for two great ladies of the end of the Seventeenth Dynasty, a mother and daughter, Aahhotep and Nefertari, were worshipped as ancestral goddesses by their descendants in the Eighteenth.   There is no break in continuity between the Seventeenth and Eighteenth Dynasties, and the matter is only of interest to Egyptologists, but between the new state of Egypt and the old feudal monarchy which we knew in the Twelfth Dynasty there is a vast gulf.

To quote Professor Erman : " The feudal state had quite disappeared and the government had become highly centralised ; the land tenure was now exactly what is described in Genesis as having been brought about by Joseph—*i.e.*, all land belonged to the king as his personal property, the people worked it and paid over one-fifth of the proceeds to the royal treasury.   All governors of provinces were appointed by the king or by the great viziers on behalf of the king, and these posts were often given as a reward for military services."   For Egypt became in this dynasty a great military power ; no doubt the army had been gathered together and the fighting habit acquired against the Hyksos, and it was very natural that the kings should use the armed force at their disposal for foreign expeditions.

King Sekenenra of the cleft skull was succeeded by Kames, who probably married Aahhotep ; their son Aahmes drove the Hyksos out of Avaris, their last stronghold in Egypt, and pursued them across the frontier to the south of Palestine.   His queen was his sister Nefertari, daughter of Aahhotep, and their son Amenhotep I. seems to have married his sister Aah-hotep II., but to have left no son, and the succession passed with their daughter Aahmes to her husband Thothmes I., who was not of royal blood.

A most beautiful and important case of jewellery, belonging to Aahhotep, Kames, and Aahmes, deserves careful study, and a comparison with the Middle Empire jewels from Dahshur will help to show some of the changes in style that had taken place in Egypt. The use of foreign designs is much more marked, is, indeed, very characteristic of the Eighteenth Dynasty.

Plate I. 2, the battle-axe of King Aahmes, is one of the most beautiful things in the magnificent collection of jewellery in Cairo, and is, moreover, of great interest as showing the influence of Mycenæan art. Indeed, the inlaid figures on it might have been made in Crete or any of the old centres of Ægean civilisation rather than in Egypt, and recall the description in Homer of the work of Hephaistos on the shield of Achilles. The gold strapping by which the blade is fixed to the handle is curious. The inlay is of gold upon bronze, and the hieroglyphs are of coloured stone let into a gold background. This Mycenæan influence is entirely to be expected, for all exploration goes to show that at this time—1600-1500 B.C.—there was a widespread civilisation round the Mediterranean, centred at Crete, which was the sea-power and carried the products of Asia Minor, Syria, Egypt, the islands and mainland of Greece from one country to another. This was the epoch of the palace at Knossos, which was several storeys in height, with frescoed walls, had a splendid throne room and modern drainage system. The tombs of Abd el Gurneh are full of pictures of foreigners and foreign wares, but in the Cairo Museum such monuments are somewhat scarce. Had the Theban private tombs only been in better preservation we should have had wonderful material for the early archæology of the Mediterranean countries, but it is only in recent years that their very great importance has been recognised, and but little has as yet been published, which amounts to saying that all the evidence they can give is in constant danger of destruction.

Thothmes I. was a really powerful king, and extended the authority of Egypt so far that the Sudan again became a province, and a great part of Syria was conquered. He even set up a memorial pillar on the shores of the Euphrates to chronicle his farthest advance to the north and east. But the records of his reign are scanty, and his main interest for us is in his family and what can be learned of their remarkable achievements, for after him there comes an extremely interesting but very difficult bit of history. There were furious quarrels about the succession, and it is impossible to be at all certain what the sequence of events really was, which is the more disappointing and makes us feel the want of literature even more keenly than usual, for assuredly there came in a question of personality and a clash of wills which must have been vivid and dramatic but at which we can only dimly guess. Professor Breasted has put forward a working hypothesis which fits in well with the known facts. According to this, Hatshepsut, Thothmes II., and Thothmes III., were all children of Thothmes I., but the only child by the queen Aahmes, through whom Thothmes I. had obtained his title to the throne, was Hatshepsut, so that she was the only divinely descended heir, and she was probably a good deal older than the two princes her half-brothers.

The Legitimist party, as we may call it, was so strong that Thothmes I., fairly early in his reign, nominated Hatshepsut as his successor in her own right, but it was an unheard-of thing for a queen to reign independently of a husband, and it was inevitable that there should be great opposition to it. It is a safe guess that Hatshepsut was a woman of talent and force of character, less safe but still probable that Thothmes II. was weak, and fairly certain that Thothmes III. was remarkably gifted.

What probably happened was that Hatshepsut married her half-brother Thothmes III. when he was a child, while Thothmes I. was still reigning. A curious scene was stage-managed in the temple of Karnak, where the young Thothmes was then acting as a priest. The image of the god, as it was being carried in solemn procession, stopped before the young prince, raised him from the ground where he had prostrated himself, and caused him to take the place where the king was wont to offer incense, thus indicating the will of the god that he should reign.

For a year or two Hatshepsut and he reigned jointly,

as it would appear by the cartouches, but Hatshepsut of course taking the entire authority; then they were in some way overcome by the opposing party, the old king Thothmes I., who associated himself with his other son Thothmes II. They took the trouble to hammer out the names of Hatshepsut on her monuments and to assert Thothmes II. as the rightful king of Egypt; but this did not last very long, for the old king died and Thothmes II. conveniently followed suit, so Hatshepsut and Thothmes III. again resumed the power, but, whether on account of Thothmes III.'s youth or the very energetic character of Hatshepsut, Thothmes remains very much in the background for several years more.

Hatshepsut found the country very prosperous and did a great deal to develop its resources by peace and good government. She did not go to war at all, and the great work of her life, after the building of her funerary temple at Der el Bahri, was the expedition she sent to Punt (S. Arabia or Somaliland?) to bring trees and herbs, gold and frankincense for the temple of her father Amen. The priesthood of Amen must have been obedient to so faithful a daughter, and there seems to have been much communication between Karnak and Der el Bahri, which, with its magnificent situation, was well suited for processions and spectacular shows such as the Egyptians loved. Happily a great deal of the temple decoration remains in place, and we can see on one whole terrace the story of her birth, and how in very truth Hatshepsut was the daughter, not of Thothmes I. the mortal, but of Amen Ra himself and the divine Queen Aahmes, and so had an unimpeachable right to the throne. These claims were taken exception to by some successor, and the names, and indeed entire figures, have been chiselled out. This irreverence has usually been set down to Thothmes III. as a posthumous revenge on Hatshepsut for having kept the reins in her own hands for so long, but it is not quite certain that it was his doing.

The principal terrace at Der el Bahri is occupied with the Punt expedition, and the pictures of ships with complicated rigging, the arrival at Punt, the barter with the inhabitants, the houses and trees of the tropical country, and the wonderful collection of things brought back to Egypt are well known and worth long study. Unfortunately many of the scenes were removed long ago, but a very good publication of all those which remain in place has been made by the Egyptian Exploration Fund. In the Cairo Museum there are only a few blocks, just enough to show the style of the work, and one of these has on it a picture of the Queen of Punt, which has the unusual quality in a museum exhibit that it may be guaranteed to make the beholder laugh (Plate X. 2). She is going in procession with figures of men of Punt carrying tribute to the Egyptians who have just arrived in the country. The artist has been at great pains to show how very fat she was and what peculiar clothes she wore. What a pity the Egyptians did not more often depart from their conventions in figure drawing! Hatshepsut says that rare and fragrant trees were brought from Punt to make beautiful the garden of Amen at Karnak and to border the roads that led to it. We have noted that her predecessor Mentuhotep had done the same long before and that the roots of the trees he planted have been covered and preserved by Hatshepsut's causeway (p. 57). There is some speculation as to how the ships went to Punt, and the probability seems to be that there was already a canal, running through the eastern Delta, which connected the Nile with the Red Sea. Such a canal certainly existed in later times, and there is a tradition (p. 65) that it was the work of Sesostris, which, considering what immense engineering works were undertaken in the Middle Empire, seems quite possible. From the pictures it certainly looks as if the ships arrived at Thebes, as they had been loaded up at Punt without any change; if they had been brought across the desert from Kosseir to Coptos we should expect to have been shown something about it.

After Hatshepsut had reigned thirty years, fifteen as heir-apparent to her father and fifteen as the wife of

Thothmes III., it was time for her to hold a jubilee festival, and the correct way to celebrate this was to set up two obelisks in the temple of the god. She sent her chancellor Senmut, with architects and an army of workmen, to carry out this and to bring larger and finer obelisks than any sovereign had yet erected. In seven months' time Senmut and his workmen quarried, shaped, inscribed, brought from Aswân, and set up in Karnak the two superb obelisks which are still in place at the entrance to the Eighteenth-Dynasty temple—one erect, the other in fragments but not beyond the possibility of being put together.

Her tomb is in the Valley of the Tombs of the Kings, where she was one of the first to be buried, and its long entrance passage is tunnelled below the cliff to a point almost underneath her temple.

After she died Thothmes was left to reign alone, and at once entered on a vigorous career of conquest. An exceptional amount is known about his time from the official annals inscribed on the walls of Karnak and from the many tombs of his generals and viziers on the Hill of Gurneh, where we can see pictures of the tribute that came from Nubia and Syria as well as read the descriptions of the campaigns abroad and records of the internal affairs of the country.

His conquests were of a much more permanent order than any that had gone before, and he evidently adapted and used several of the Syrian coast towns as military and naval bases where his fleet could lie in safety and he could gather his stores for expeditions by land. He made no less than seventeen campaigns in Syria, laid most of the peoples of Palestine under tribute, and settled Egyptian officials as local governors in several places. As he went northwards and inland he came in contact with two powerful non-Semitic peoples who inhabited the northern Euphrates valley—the Mitanni, who seem to have had their capital somewhere in the region of Aleppo, and the Hittites, who were beginning to push down from Asia Minor. Thothmes III. crossed the Euphrates, defeated the Mitanni, and even made a treaty with the King of Babylon, but of course made no permanent acquisition of territory so far away from Egypt. Besides this vast activity in Syria he made one or two expeditions into the Sudan, where the frontier of Egypt was always having to be pushed farther south, and the claim in his annals that the boundaries of his empire were from the Fourth Cataract of the Nile to Euphrates was probably well justified.

Thebes must have been a marvellous place in his time, with boats and barges of every size and description coming and going with the wealth of the Mediterranean lands and the abundance of gold and ivory, slaves, incense, and furs from the Sudan. Lions, apes, and giraffes were brought to stock the gardens of the king and his father Amen, and horses and chariots, unknown to ancient times, came down in great numbers from Syria as trophies of war. Horses were apparently brought in by the Hyksos from Asia; at least, there is no mention of them in the Middle Empire, whereas at the beginning of the Eighteenth Dynasty they are frequently shown on the tomb walls and very well drawn.

On the hill of Sheikh Abd el Gurneh are the graves of the men who carried on the works of building and decorating the temples, who brought down the obelisks from the quarries, superintended the collection of tribute from foreigners and taxes from Egyptians, and as the art of the Eighteenth Dynasty was extremely faithful and graphic the interest of studying these representations is unparalleled. When the artists could let themselves go a little and were not too much hampered by the strict canons of orthodox tomb decoration we get most spirited pictures, and they specially enjoyed drawing anything which was new to them, like the long, embroidered robe of Hittites and other Asiatics and the beautiful shapes of the gold and silver vases that came from Europe. High up, near the top of the hill, is the tomb of old Anena, who held office under Thothmes I., II., and III.; not far off is that of Senmut, Hatshepsut's trusted chancellor and steward. It must have been deliberately destroyed by the action of enemies in ancient times, for its walls are chipped away with regular and systematic thoroughness except in one corner, where a little row of four figures still remains, and by good luck these are no ordinary offering bearers, but show the narrow waists drawn tightly in by a girdle of coloured leather which we have learned to know as Cretan; moreover, they carry vases with Mycenæan ornament, and one of them even

CRETANS.

bears a silver cup adorned with bulls' heads and gold rosettes, which must assuredly have come from the Knossos Palace. In the fourth Egyptian room of the British Museum are several fine fragments of wall-painting from these tombs, which give a good idea of the subjects and the technique used by the artists. They are not quite so good as the best, but they are very charming and show several interesting scenes. There is a beautiful one where Sebekhotep, the owner of the tomb, goes out into the marshes in a little boat to boomerang the birds. His wife stands by him, a small daughter squatting in the bottom of the boat clasps his knees, and his retrieving cat, climbing up a papyrus stem which bends under its weight, catches the wounded birds.   Other scenes represent the inspection of geese and cattle, which was probably conducted in the very same way as we were shown it in the Eleventh Dynasty in Plate VII., only here it is painted on a flat wall instead of being modelled in the round.   One of the most interesting of these frescoes has a scene of the bringing in of tribute by Syrians whose dress and features are very characteristic and are often to be seen in the Sheikh el Gurneh tombs. Another fragment shows the painting of a garden with a large pond in the middle, all drawn according to Egyptian rules and a little difficult to understand at first, but this and all the other frescoes are most interesting and worthy of study.

One of the most important of these tombs is that of Rekhmara, a vizier under Thothmes III., but unfortunately it has been much copied, and the copyists have, as at Beni Hassan, treated it with some medium which has damaged the colours very much; the light is not very good, and considerable time must be allowed there if one is to get an adequate notion of the variety of subjects and the excellence of the work.   On the wall facing the doorway, on the left-hand side, is a fine representation of the products of the Sudan, and not only are the piles of ivory tusks and rings of gold depicted and numbered as they were placed in the treasury, but we see a live elephant being brought along, a bear, a baboon, and a giraffe with a monkey clinging to its long neck. Chariots and prancing horses come from Syria as well as fine vases, bows and arrows, jewellery, and other things of value.   In the inner part are all details of the funeral ceremonies, including the making of furniture and statues, the banquet with guests wreathed in lotus flowers; also singers and dancers, but these are of frequent occurrence and can be better studied in other tombs.   The drawing of negro women with their babies is from the tomb of Huy, a Viceroy of the Sudan.   The colouring is bright and crude, the petticoats being striped red, blue, and yellow.   This tomb is full of interesting

scenes and pictures of animals, boats, and objects im-
ported from Nubia, but it is difficult to see, as, like many
other of the rock tombs, it was used as a house until
recent times, and some of the paintings are so blackened

NUBIAN WOMEN.

by smoke as to be in a hopeless condition. A large part
of it has been beautifully copied—and so rescued from
complete destruction—by Mrs. de Garis Davies.

The mortuary temple of Thothmes III. was on the
edge of the desert, looking to Thebes, but it is in total
ruin, and for the finest work directly carried out by him

we must look to Karnak, where he did a great deal of building, much of which remains and is sufficient to give us a fair idea of the size and appearance of the temple at this period.

We have to " think away " the Hypostyle Hall and all the forecourt near the Nile and then stand facing the Eighteenth-Dynasty temple of which Thothmes built the great hall and a pylon; his, too, are the lovely granite columns with lotus and papyrus ornament—symbolic of Upper and Lower Egypt—and among the most curious and interesting parts of Karnak is the festival hall, built for his Sed Heb festival (held to celebrate his jubilee year, the first occasion after a reign of thirty years, possibly every fifth year of his reign after that), with its garden adjoining, and on the walls of one little hall a list of the flowers, trees, and animals which he had brought from his Syrian campaigns to enrich the temple of his father Amen Ra. These things still stand in Karnak, in the place for which they were made, but the obelisks he set up for his many jubilees are scattered far and wide. One is in Constantinople, one in Rome, one on the Thames Embankment, and one in Central Park, New York.

Many of his portraits exist; the best of them is a beautiful statue of him as a young man (Plate IV. 3, Cairo Museum). It is carved in dark-coloured slate and was found at Karnak along with many other statues which had been thrown into a pit below water level and were laboriously recovered not many years ago. This is another of the temple *caches* like that in the old temple at Hieraconpolis (p. 12), and probably means that the statues were hurriedly swept out of the way of the Assyrians, who devastated the place under Assurbanipal.

The tomb of Thothmes III. is not often visited; the approach to it is steep and the descent into it somewhat difficult. It is hidden away among the cliffs at the head of the valley, and, being so remote, has not been lighted by electricity, so it would not be one of those seen on a single visit, but it is a remarkable place with a great oval hall inside covered with a fine decoration in black line like that in the tomb of his successor Amenhotep II. It is not surprising that such a king as Thothmes III. should have become a god to succeeding generations in a more literal sense than the formal deification which was decreed to every Pharaoh. He was a popular hero as well as a great king, and hundreds of years after his death his name was such a lucky thing to have about one that scarab amulets bearing his name are among the commonest of Egyptian antiquities.

The tomb of Amenhotep II. is a very interesting one. It was discovered some years ago, and happily the mummy had not been removed in ancient times, but was found in place in the splendid quartzite sarcophagus where it still lies, and the electric lamp of the twentieth century now sheds its light on the very features of the Pharaoh in the very place where he was laid to rest 3,400 years ago.

His jewellery had been plundered by the ancient robbers and the tomb ransacked for anything of value, but the fragments that were left still make a goodly show in the Cairo Museum, where they are arranged along with the very similar relics of his successor Thothmes IV. The pieces of glass from these tombs are interesting specimens of a very early technique, and specially to be noted is a magnificent chariot front from the war chariot of Thothmes IV., which has been placed in the south gallery, near the model of a complete chariot from the Florence Museum. It is ornamented with scenes of the king riding over the prostrate forms of his Syrian and negro foes, whose characteristic features are most admirably drawn. When covered, as it originally was, with paint and gilding this must have been a superb piece.

This king, Thothmes IV., comes before us in another connection besides that of the objects from his tomb. It is a long while since we have heard much of Memphis, but he seems to have spent some time in that part of Egypt, and is said to have made the first attempt on record to clear the Great Sphinx of sand. One day, while he was still a prince and perhaps not heir to the throne, he was hunting on the desert near Giza and fell asleep in the shadow of the Sphinx. He does not make any mention of the pyramids, and believed the Sphinx to be an image of his father the sun-god, under which aspect it was worshipped at that time. In a dream his father, the god, appeared to him and promised him the kingdom and a long reign if he would do to him that which he desired and remove the sand of the desert from his aching limbs. The prince was obedient to the vision, cleared away the sand, and set up a tablet between the paws to tell the tale. A stela, professing to be an ancient copy of this tablet, still stands there, now entirely covered by the sand. It should be noted that the word " stela " had by this time extended its meaning so far as to include purely secular objects. Any single stone with figures and inscription commemorative of an historical event is known as a stela. It is hardly necessary to add that the *funerary* stela was still the essential part of tomb decoration, although somewhat modified in character.

An important event for Egyptian history was the marriage of Thothmes IV. with a princess of the Mitanni, Mut em Ua. This was the first of many foreign alliances, and marks the beginning of a change in Egyptian manners also; as we shall see in the following chapter, it made an irregularity in the succession which had to be got over by a new intervention of Amen Ra.

CHAPTER VIII

NEW EMPIRE (Continued): LATER EIGHTEENTH DYNASTY

(1411–1350 B.C.)

AMENHOTEP III. succeeded his father Thothmes IV., but as he was the son of a foreign princess and not of an Egyptian heiress to the throne, this was not in the regular order of things according to received ideas, and Amenhotep III., one of the most powerful and magnificent of Egyptian kings, seems not to have been one of those who had the best title to the throne.

In this reign Egypt was at the zenith of its power, and Amenhotep aimed at consolidating its greatness, not by further foreign conquest, but by peaceful alliances and development at home. Thebes, the capital, was to be more splendid than ever, and Amen was to be worshipped on an even greater scale than before. It was doubtless, however, for dynastic reasons that he felt the need of building a new and special temple for the god, in which could be incorporated another scene of "divine birth," similar to the one in Der el Bahri, where Hatshepsut proclaims her legitimate right to the throne of Egypt as being the daughter of Amen Ra. Amenhotep built the colonnaded court of the temple of Luxor, which many consider to be the highest achievement of Egyptian architecture, and in one of the small chambers adjoining it, generally known as the Birth House, he adapts the story of the divine birth to legitimise his own claim to be king, through his mother Mut em Ua, whom Amen Ra is supposed to have seen, loved, and gained possession of by the help of Isis. The treatment of the tale is almost exactly similar to that at Der el Bahri; the fashioning of

95

the child and his "Ka" by Khnum, the goddesses attending on Mut em Ua at his birth, his presentation to Amen, and being nursed by the nine Hathors in the presence of the gods. The British Museum preserves several of his portraits, two of which, in hard sandstone, are especially fine and must have come from his funerary temple.

Amenhotep III. also built extensively at Karnak and made the great avenue of sphinxes which connected the two temples and along which the sacred barque of the god was borne in procession on his festival days. But, in spite of all this tremendous show of devotion to Amen and the established ritual of Egyptian religion, there were opposing forces at work, and the breath of a new spirit was inspiring the ancient traditions with a new life.

Here we find ourselves at an extremely interesting point of history, for the next half-century was to decide whether Egypt should take its place—the leading place, as it would then have been—among the young civilisations that were rising in the other countries round the Mediterranean seaboard. It felt the new spirit stirring, it touched new heights of thought, new aims in art, but the weight of the past was too heavy, and before the Eighteenth Dynasty closed Egypt's future was sealed and its religion and art stereotyped for all time. Other nations were making rapid progress about this time, for a very different state of things appears in Syria in the Eighteenth Dynasty from what is known of it from the few mentions which occur earlier. And Syrian influence was enormous in Egypt at the time of Amenhotep III. The tombs are full of pictures of the beautiful things that came from there and from Crete, and we may be sure that the king and the great nobles took the pride of collectors in the graceful vases, the gold and silver inlaid work, and embroideries that came from abroad.

The foreign influence in this reign is so strong that the famous wife of Amenhotep III., Queen Thyi, was often supposed to have been a foreigner, but the discovery of the tomb of her parents, Yuaa and Thuaa, has shown that to all appearance they were Egyptians, and not of the royal house, so that her revolutionary views, as well as her great importance in the history of Egypt, remain something of a puzzle. She must have been a very remarkable woman indeed. Amenhotep associated her with himself on nearly all his monuments, and his and her colossal statues are the first things that catch the eye as we enter the museum of Cairo. These were made for their funerary temple which stood on the edge of the desert, now under cultivation, behind the two large Colossi which all travellers pass on their way to the Ramesseum and Medinet Habu. These are, indeed, colossal statues of Amenhotep III. which stood in front of his temple and were famous in Roman time as the Colossi of Memnon. Amenhotep had a palace not far from there and made a great artificial lake on which he and Queen Thyi went boating. It is almost certain that the mounds of the Birket Habu, a little to the south of the Colossi, were part of the enclosing embankment of this artificial sheet of water.

Extensive remains of the palace are still to be seen, but they only show the ground plan consisting of low lines of brick walls, and it requires a patient study of these and of the fragments that were carefully gathered up in the course of excavations to restore the place and the scheme of decoration, which was extremely gay and brilliant. Aided also by the palace of Akhenaten, the son of Amenhotep III., at Tell el Amarna, which is similar in style, it has been possible to reconstruct the patterns on ceilings, floors, columns, and door jambs. The brick walls were covered with a fine coating of white plaster on which were painted flowers, birds, and fish, very free and broad in treatment; some of the floors represented a pond fringed with water-plants with lotus growing from it, fish swimming, and birds flying. This kind of ornament would doubtless soon wear off, but must have been cheap and easy to replace. On one at least of the roofs was the pattern, well known in Crete, of spirals and

7

bulls' heads; round the doors was another design of spirals, here carried out in gold leaf and tiles of gorgeous blue faience. New York Museum will some day show a reconstruction of one of the halls of this palace, which will be of the utmost interest, and at present exhibits some of the objects and *motifs* of decoration which were found there.

As to the plan of the building, there were two or three large halls for banquets or audiences, and apparently much open-air accommodation on loggias and roofs, but the most novel and interesting feature to us is the private apartments of the courtiers and ladies-in-waiting, perhaps the ladies of the royal *harîm*. There are many suites of these, divided by corridors running lengthwise, then by short cross-passages, from each of which open two sets of rooms. Each of the suites consists of two bedrooms, a sitting-room, maid's room, and bathroom; at least, that is how we should express it in modern times if similar plans were to be seen in a building. The bath is not in a tub, but in a room with a slightly sloping floor, like an Egyptian bathroom of the present day, so that the water, when poured out of a jar, ran off down a little drain into a tank outside the room, from whence it was emptied by servants.

We can form an idea of the furniture that was used in such a palace from the very fine and complete set of funerary equipment which was found in the tomb of the father and mother of Queen Thyi.

By good fortune this tomb had remained untouched since about 1200 B.C., when two neighbouring tombs had been hollowed out of the rock and the stone chip and débris from them thrown over the opening of the modest little shaft that led to the tomb of Yuaa and Thuaa. Its walls were undecorated; it was simply a small, rough chamber hewn in the rock, but the dark little cavern was filled with beautiful furniture and gleamed with gold and silver from the overlaying of the coffins and the panelling of beds and chairs. Only the jewels had been taken by the robbers who had penetrated there in ancient times. These had indeed done their work with haste and roughness, for coffin lids were wrenched away and thrown heedlessly aside, and wrappings torn from the bodies to get the quicker at their golden ornaments; but later the mass of chips piled on above protected the grave, and what the old Egyptian thieves left has proved to be the greatest find of funerary furniture that has ever come to light, for nearly all the objects were of the choicest workmanship and had besides a distinctive quality about them as of something personally thought out.

Every visitor to Cairo Museum sees and enjoys these things, and even a hurried survey will not fail to show that they are very beautiful, and, as is so often said, "so modern," but they will more than repay very close examination, for in regard to even the most conventional of the funeral necessaries, such as Canopic jars and *ushabtiu* figures, there is some novel feature. The Canopic jars in themselves are fine specimens of the ordinary type, but in the case of the lady Thuaa's Canopics the internal organs placed in the jar were carefully mummified, bandaged, shaped out by the addition of little pads to the form of a sort of doll mummy, and then set in the jar with a little mask of gold cartonnage over the head.

The *ushabtiu* are a particularly dainty set; all are different in size, shape, and material, each was provided with a little upright case like a sentry-box, and instead of the usual tools and bag painted on the figures these have little model tools made of wood and copper. The larger pieces of furniture, beds, chairs, and tables, are charmingly designed, the pattern of the ornament (Plate XIII.) on the chariot apron is worth some attention as it is entirely Mycenæan in character; the coffins, too, with their inlay of precious stones, are the finest of their kind, and the mummies themselves seem to preserve more individuality than is usually seen; probably the process was carried out with even greater care and expense than was generally bestowed.

In the Turin Museum are the complete contents of an unplundered tomb of this period which are in most extraordinarily fine condition. Unfortunately, as they are not

yet published, there is no way of getting to know anything more about them, except the not always convenient
method of going to Turin, but anyone who has the opportunity of seeing them ought by no means to miss the
chance.

The contents of the tomb are arranged in a small room,
approximately of the size and shape of the chamber
where they were found, the low doorway is closed by
the original wooden door of the tomb, and the first sight
which meets the eye on entering is a bed spread with
sheets and a fringed coverlet of fine linen. The offerings
that were laid on the table in the Eighteenth Dynasty
are there to this day; loaves of bread, bunches of onions,
lumps of fat, flowers; all these most perishable things
are still to be looked on, though how many palaces and
empires have passed away since they were closed up in
the grave at Thebes! The secret of their wonderful
escape from the ever-industrious robber was probably
that the tomb did not contain any jewellery, so was not
considered worth plundering by contemporary thieves
and was overlooked by the modern searchers after tomb
furniture.

But the objects are very fine, only a little less beautiful
than those from the famous tomb of Yuaa and Thuaa in
the Cairo Museum, while the preservation of the food
offerings is unequalled elsewhere.

We should expect that the tombs of Amenhotep and
Thyi themselves would be the most magnificent of all,
but here disappointment awaits us, for however splendid
the tomb of Amenhotep may have been it was completely
plundered in antiquity. It is situated in the west branch
of the valley and is rather difficult of access. Queen
Thyi's tomb and all the question of her burial is one of
the still unsolved puzzles of history. She was probably
buried at Tell el Amarna and her mummy subsequently
brought back to Thebes, but the few relics of tomb furniture which have been ascribed to her are uncertain and
seem inadequate to her great position. The only certain
portrait of her is the colossal statue along with her
husband, but her figure often appears in groups with

him and his mother, and she is frequently mentioned in inscriptions as "the great royal wife."

During the reign of Amenhotep III. a change is noticeable in art in the direction of realism and the discarding of convention, influenced no doubt by the vigorous art of Crete, for though it is probable that the sack of Knossos and the destruction of the sea-power of Crete happened about this time, that would be rather in favour of the idea that artists escaping from its ruin should have come to Egypt. Egyptian articles, especially scarabs, are fairly often found on Mycenæan sites in Europe, dated to Amenhotep and Thyi.

But no outside influence will account for the extraordinary change in ideas and beliefs which took place under their son Amenhotep IV., or, as he afterwards called himself, Akhenaten, Khuenaten, or Ikhnaton, as it is variously written. His religious revolution has long been known and used to be attributed entirely to himself, but the discovery of his mummy not many years ago provided one of the disturbing facts which now and again crop up to overturn theories of Egyptian history just when they seem to be really well established.

Anatomical examination was made and irrefutable evidence showed that the body was that of a young man, not over twenty-eight years of age. Now Akhenaten is known to have reigned seventeen years, and the religious revolution took place at an early period of his reign, so if he succeeded at the age of eleven, for the first few years he must have been under the control of his mother, who acted as regent, and this seems to show that Thyi was quite as much of a reformer as her son. It is just possible that the mummy is not that of Akhenaten, but this is hardly open to question, for it lay in his coffin in a tomb only occupied by relics of him and his mother—and it certainly was not Queen Thyi. Moreover, his death at the early age of twenty-seven or twenty-eight does *just* allow time for the known events of his reign; his marriage at fifteen would not be unlikely, and his daughters are always shown as little girls.

These few years of the young king's reign are unique

in ancient history. His lifework was for freedom, freedom of religious thought from the bonds of idolatry, freedom for the State from the trammels of a priesthood. The priests of Amen must have been arrogant as medieval popes; they held vast wealth which had been showered on them by Akhenaten's predecessors, besides the spiritual power they wielded over the Theban people; but this wonderful boy and his mother broke through it all and declared that Amen Ra and all the gods were but idols dumb and there was one God above all and through all and in us all, who could not be represented by the image of earthly things. They went back to Heliopolis to find the purest and least material form in which this deity could be worshipped, and they chose the Aten—the sun's disc—or rather the power emanating from it, as the manifestation of the divine being best suited for the adoration of mankind.

Such a far-reaching change could not be carried through at Thebes, with temples of Amen all around, a disaffected priesthood, and a people brought up in un-questioning reverence for the old religion. So the new order of things required a new city and new temples, and accordingly a new city and new temples were built. This new town was called Akhet Aten, and is now known as Tell el Amarna; it lies nearly opposite to the village of Deirout in Middle Egypt.

Tell el Amarna is a remarkable town, and as it was situated on the desert, unlike most Egyptian cities, and only inhabited during a very short period, objects found there can be dated with precision. It was built on a wide, flat stretch of desert, so little above the cultivation level that every house had a garden and well adjoining, and as the site afforded unlimited space for expansion it was laid out in a most spacious manner.

There were apparently no regular streets, but a suc-cession of villas, large and small, with open spaces surrounding them, and covering thus a very large extent of ground compared to the population. The place could have been built very rapidly, for we know how quickly brick houses are run up in Egypt, and the regular wall-decoration at that time was floral or animal ornament, free and unconventional in design, and very rapid, almost careless, in execution. Part of the palace pavement, now in Cairo Museum, is a good example of this style of work, but, as we have seen from the palace of Amenhotep III., a few years earlier in date, the naturalistic movement was already fully in vogue before the removal to Tell el Amarna.

To Tell el Amarna Akhenaten moved with all his court, and for a few short years the new religion reigned supreme : everything that had to do with the worship of Amen was abomination, and first of all the royal name had to be purified from it, so the king, who had succeeded as Amenhotep IV., changed his name and called himself by that of the god he worshipped, Akhenaten, or the "glory of the Aten." Not content with this, he caused the name of Amen to be effaced from the cartouches of his father wherever they were to be found. This, of course, was not done with absolute thoroughness, but cases of it are frequently to be seen. Take, for instance, a fine stela in the Eighteenth Dynasty room in Cairo (Plate XI.), which was dedicated by Amenhotep III. to commemorate his victories over Syrians and Negroes. At the top the king is seen making offerings to Amen Ra, while below he drives his chariot over the conquered enemies. Notice the cartouches. Those which had "Amen" in them have been chipped out and the figure of the god defaced. This was the work of Akhenaten's iconoclasts. But some years later, when Amen had come back to his own and more than ever was the great god, Seti I., a very devout worshipper, set himself to repair the sacrilege of Akhenaten in as many places as he could, so we see here how the cartouche has been carved in again on the roughened surface caused by the previous chipping out. And the incised inscription in the middle of the stela was put there by Seti, to say that he had done this for the sake of his father Amen Ra.

One of the most interesting of the Gurneh tombs is that of Rames or Ramose, who was vizier during the change from the worship of Amen to that of the Aten, for on one side of his tomb door the king is called Amenhotep and on the other Akhenaten. On either side the king is shown seated on the throne, under a canopy symbolising the palace, and as Akhenaten he is represented with the rays of the sun descending on him and shedding life on earth. The decoration on this part of the tomb behind the figure of the king is only in outline and seems to have been soon abandoned, but the drawing is characteristic of the Tell el Amarna style. The other and more complete side of the colonnaded forecourt contains some most beautiful work. This tomb, being on the low ground below the Sheikh Abd el Gurneh hill, seems to have struck on a vein of rock of a better quality than is found higher up, so it was possible to carve some of the decoration in relief, and no one who cares for the beauty of pure line can fail to enjoy some of the charming work in this and in the neighbouring tomb of Kha em Hayt. There is very little in Egyptian or any other art that can challenge comparison with the best of the Italian Renaissance, but at the far end of the excavated part of the tomb of Ramose are two panels, each containing the figure of a boy carrying flowers, which almost irresistibly carry our thoughts to Florence and Donatello. Plate XII. shows a typical stela of Akhenaten, where he and his queen are standing in adoration before the Aten, the sun's disc, from which the rays pour down.

Some of the finest pieces from the tomb of Kha em Hayt have unhappily been stolen and sold to Berlin Museum, where they lose much of their beauty being torn from their surroundings, but one or two very choice bits are still in place, and casts have been made from the blocks in Berlin and set up in the tomb, which makes the scenes more intelligible. He was superintendent of granaries under Amenhotep III., and most of the scenes are concerned with the bringing in and cataloguing of the cattle and grain—not a subject of deep interest, but treated in most delicate low relief. But most of the tombs of this period are at Tell el Amarna and have suffered very much from " reprisals " by the Amen priesthood after his restoration. Happily a good many portraits of the king Akhenaten exist, as well as several stelæ on which he is depicted as receiving gifts and power from the Aten. The sun's rays are represented as ending in hands showering gifts over Akhenaten and his family. These are quite characteristic and unlike any other monuments (Plate XII.).

The extraordinary figures of the king and queen cannot pass without comment, and certainly most of them show a realism run mad. Probably the taste in art was so novel that only the very best artists succeeded and the others fell into caricature. But it is only fair to judge of any period by its best, and here the best is very startlingly good. Akhenaten seems almost to have overleapt two millenniums and to have anticipated medieval Europe rather than classic Greece, for his portraits have none of the regular beauty and complacent dignity of Thothmes or Rameses, to say nothing of Greek sculpture, but they are full of dreaminess, of suffering—in a word, of soul.

The finest of them is in Berlin Museum, but there is enough in Cairo to bear out what has been said. A most interesting collection of studies and fragments from a sculptor's studio at Tell el Amarna is contained in the Eighteenth Dynasty room. These show great freshness in subject. What other king of Egypt would have allowed himself to be represented playing with his children and kissing a little daughter who sits on his lap? Artists will note the modelling of lips and eyelids in some of the little heads in this case. The exquisite set of Canopic jars with portrait heads can hardly belong to anyone but the king; they are their own best evidence, for they are unmistakably like the best of his portraits. Three of the four are in Cairo (the finest of these is shown in Plate X. 1), and the remaining one is in the Metropolitan Museum of New York. They are of alabaster, unpainted save for the eyes and the inlaid eyebrows, and the soft, creamy stone has lent itself well to the extreme delicacy of the modelling. Very seldom in the ancient world does Art endeavour to express more than beauty of form, but in looking at this head we scarcely stop to think whether it is beautiful or not, so full it is of inward beauty of the spirit.

The coffin of Akhenaten is a highly ornate piece of work, covered with inlay of lapis-lazuli, carnelian, and blue glaze. This style of decoration was begun on his grandfather Yuaa's coffin, but there it is confined to the hieroglyphic inscription and the necklace, and the effect is more pleasing than on that of Akhenaten, which seems decidedly overloaded. The coffin, or rather the coffin lid, is in Cairo Museum. The large piece of painted pavement in the middle of the museum comes from his palace at Tell el Amarna; it is very good and broad in the treatment of flowers and birds, but this is paralleled by the scraps of a similar pavement from his father's palace at Thebes.

During the reigns of both these kings there was constant traffic with Syria, and a regular correspondence went on with several of the kings and chiefs of Asia from as far as the Orontes and Euphrates. A good many of these princes had been vassals of Egypt since the time of Thothmes III., but it is curious that their letters were not written in Egyptian, but in the Babylonian language in the wedge-shaped characters known as cuneiform, and that they are not written on papyrus, but in the Babylonian way, on little clay tablets about the size and shape of cakes of soap. A large number of these were found at Tell el Amarna and must have formed part of the archives of Akhenaten. They are very important historical documents, but perhaps their chief interest to many people will be the fact that in them there is much complaint of a people called the Khabiri, who were attacking Palestine from the east and harrying all the country. If it should be the case that the Children of Israel left Egypt early in the Eighteenth Dynasty, this might very well be the account of their arrival in Palestine, corresponding to that in the Book of Joshua, only giving the other side. And a period when the Egyptian rule had become slack seems a not unlikely time for this

to have happened, for even under Amenhotep III. the
control was somewhat relaxed, and Akhenaten evidently
did not attempt to keep up the foreign empire of
Thothmes III.; perhaps he simply did not have time,
for we can hardly suppose that a man who built a new
capital and introduced a new religion before he was
twenty-six could have managed to carry on a career of
conquest as well. And such a foreign empire, as Egypt's
was, had to be continually kept going by warlike expeditions, and there was never any idea of federation or
absorption; moreover, another enemy was threatening
Syria about this time from the north—namely, the
Hittites, a non-Semitic people who came down from Asia
Minor, probably from the highlands of Armenia, so, by
the end of the reign of Akhenaten, Egyptian authority in
Syria was practically lost.

The cemetery of Tell el Amarna, where many of
Akhenaten's noblemen and ministers are buried, is near
the town, but the grave of Akhenaten himself is hidden
away in a remote valley four hours' ride from the river.
Some of his family were buried there, and he and his
mother were most likely laid there also and afterwards
taken secretly away to Thebes, to escape the destruction
which was carried out on everything relating to the Aten
worship when the reaction came. The tombs of his
courtiers at Tell el Amarna were savagely mutilated, but
from what remains several interesting and beautiful
scenes have been recovered, and the famous Hymn to
the Aten, collated from two or three different versions
which were written out in the tombs. This poem is of
so high a literary quality, and confirms so well the
claims made for Akhenaten's great step forward in
religious thought, that it seems desirable to quote from
it at some length :

" Beautiful is thy resplendent appearing in heaven,
    O living Aten, who art the beginning of life.
  When thou ascendest in the eastern horizon, thou fillest every
      land with thy beauties.
  Thou art fair and great, radiant, high above all the earth,

Thy beams encompass the lands to the sum of all that thou hast
created.
Thou subduest them with thy love.
Though thou art afar, thy beams are upon the earth.
Thou art in the sky and day followeth thy steps.
When thou settest on the western horizon of heaven
The land is in darkness like unto death :
They sleep in their chambers,
Their heads are covered, their nostrils are closed,
    The eye seeth not his fellow.
All their goods are stolen from under their heads and they know
it not.
Every lion cometh forth out of its cave; all creeping things bite.
The earth is silent and He that made it resteth on his horizon.
When at dawn thou uprisest and shinest as Aten
Darkness flees, thou givest forth thy rays, the two lands are in
festival day by day.
They wake and stand upon their feet, for thou hast raised them.
Their limbs are purified, they clothe themselves with their
garments.
Their hands are uplifted in adoration at thy rising,
The whole land goeth about its several labours.
Flocks rest in their pastures,
Trees and plants grow green,
Birds fly forth from their nests,
All flocks leap upon their feet,
All flying things and all hovering things, they live when thou
risest upon them.
Ships pass down stream and pass up stream likewise,
Every way is open at thy rising.
The fishes in the river leap up before thee,
Thy rays are within the great waters.
It is thou who causest women to be fruitful, men to beget.
Thou quickenest the child in its mother's womb,
Thou soothest it that it cry not,
Thou dost nurture it within its mother's womb,
Thou givest breath to cause all its functions to live,
It cometh forth from the womb upon the day of its birth,
Thou openest its mouth that it may speak, thou providest for all
its wants.
Then there is a chick within an egg, cheeping as it were, within
a stone ;
Thou givest it breath therein to cause thy handiwork to live.
It is full formed when it breaketh through the shell,
It runneth on its feet when it cometh out thence.
How manifold are thy works,
O one God who hast no fellow.
Thou createdst the earth according to thy will, when thou wast
alone.
Its people, its herds and all flocks,

All that is on earth going upon feet, all that is on high and
   flieth with wings,
The countries of Syria, of Ethiopia, of Egypt.
Thou makest the Nile in the deep, thou bringest it at thy
   pleasure
That it may give life to men, even as thou hast made them for
   thyself.
O Lord of them all, who art outwearied for them,
O Lord of earth who risest for them,
O Aten of day that risest over distant countries,
   Thou makest their life.
Thou placest the Nile in heaven, that it may descend to them,
That it may rise in waves upon the rocks like the sea,
Watering their fields and their villages.
How excellent are thy ways, O Lord of eternity.
A Nile in heaven poureth down for nations,
But the Nile cometh from the deep to the land of Egypt.
The whole earth is in thy hand even as thou hast made it,
At thy rising all live, at thy setting they die.''

There is nothing like this in Egyptian literature;
indeed, there is nothing like it in any literature until
Homer, and nothing comparable to it in spiritual insight
until centuries later, when the Hebrew prophets and
psalmists praised Jehovah. The passage in the last
stanza quoted, about the '' Nile in heaven,'' is interesting, as it gives an exact parallel to the '' waters above
the firmament '' in Genesis, and evidently is a natural
way of explaining rainfall.

Akhenaten's changes were very short-lived; apparently
they depended entirely on his personality and had no
effect at all on Egyptian thought, for even in the time of
his son-in-law and successor the tide of reaction was
flowing fast, and the nation seems to have gone back to
the Amen worship with delight. This king reversed the
process gone through by his father-in-law and changed
his name, which at first had been Tutankhaten, to Tutankhamen, took the royal residence back to Thebes, and
henceforward Tell el Amarna was abandoned and the
religious revolution had come to an end.

But since the discovery of his tomb in December, 1922,
Tutankhamen has sprung into a world-wide fame such as
never before fell to the lot of any Pharaoh, and the pains-

taking archæologists who are trying to preserve his beautiful furniture have to work in a blaze of publicity that never shone before on antiquarian pursuits.

It is not easy, among the multitude of objects, to select for description what will be of the most abiding interest or to judge how much it will be possible to exhibit at an early date, but a few general remarks may assist the reader, even now, to understand the place of the Carnarvon "find" in Egyptian art, and may, perhaps, have some permanent value after the things are displayed.

Firstly, it is not a *new* art; it is the art of Tell el Amarna, one of the best-known, as it is one of the most interesting, periods. Further, the things are, as was to be expected, very like those in the tomb of Yuaa and Thuaa, the grandparents of Akhenaten, only there are far more of them, and they are finer things. The tomb of Tutankhamen, like theirs, had been robbed very soon after the burial, and at that time it was only the jewellery and objects of solid gold that were worth stealing. This happy accident was due in both cases to the fact that the chips from the excavation of a later tomb were thrown out over the opening and thus protected the gorgeous store of furniture. The condition of most of the objects is good, but some, especially the textiles, are in a very fragile state and require a great deal of treatment before they can be safely removed.

The historical importance of the discovery is probably not very great, but it is rather too soon to affirm anything positively about this. Several objects are inscribed with both the names of the king—that of Tutankhaten, as he was called while he reigned at Tell el Amarna, and Tutankhamen, which he assumed when he returned to Thebes and the old Amen worship. This may mean that he tried to effect a compromise between the two religions and wished to establish the cult of Aten at Thebes along with that of Amen Ra, but whether further examination of the tomb will do anything to solve this question, or simply raise it, is still uncertain.

Among the choicest things are four superb alabaster vases with delicately carved handles, a box, painted on one side of the lid with a scene of Tutankhamen hunting lions, on the other side with a desert landscape, and down the sides with battle scenes, all on a scale of miniature-like fineness of execution ; also a great " throne " or chair of state, which appears to have been a real piece of palace furniture and not a model made for the tomb. These and some others are novelties of the greatest interest, for nothing approaching them in artistic merit has been seen before; but the bulk of the furniture found in the first chamber seems to be of the well-known Eighteenth-Dynasty type, only richer and more varied than anything found hitherto.

Little is known of the two or three kings who followed, but a prominent figure in history is King Horemheb, who is placed by some authorities at the end of the Eighteenth Dynasty, by others at the beginning of the Nineteenth, but does not seem to have been connected with either family. He legalised his position by marriage with a high priestess of Amen, and as he was a good soldier and an energetic administrator he did much to set right the affairs of the nation, which had fallen into considerable confusion after the revolution of Akhenaten. Artistically his monuments have still something of the inspiration which glows in those of Tell el Amarna, though he was a faithful son of Amen. The beautiful statue of Khonsu in the Eighteenth Dynasty room in Cairo Museum may be a portrait of him, and his tomb in the valley has an unusual sort of decoration in very bright colour. A good deal of his work is to be seen at Karnak, where he probably designed the great Hypostyle Hall.

Before he became king he was in some high position at Memphis, and had even got ready a tomb at Sakkara, which was never occupied, but not much is known about his private life.

The illustration on p. 112 shows part of a very charming scene of musicians at the banquet in the next world from the tomb of Nekht, which dates from about the end of the Eighteenth or beginning of the Nineteenth Dynasty and has all the character of that time. One can see strong influence of the realism of Tell el Amarna in the flowing, easy lines and in the rather daring piece of drawing which shows the nude girl with her breasts in full front view. This is a breaking away from the convention that

MUSICIANS FROM TOMB OF NEKHT.

is very unusual in Egyptian art. The whole tomb, which is beautiful and remarkable for the brilliant preservation of its colour, has been magnificently published by the Metropolitan Museum of New York.

CHAPTER IX

NEW EMPIRE (Continued): NINETEENTH DYNASTY

(1350–1205 B.C.)

THIS dynasty begins either with Horemheb, as was mentioned at the end of the last chapter, or with Rameses I., about whom very little is known and whose title to the throne must have come through his wife. Monuments of his short reign are rare, but New York possesses an important set of very fine reliefs from a temple of Osiris, founded or restored by him at Abydos. He was an old man at the time of his accession, and in the first or second year of his reign he associated with him in the government his son Seti, of whom there is much to be said.

Although in comparison with the beautiful Eighteenth-Dynasty work the characteristic of Nineteenth-Dynasty art is rather size than elegance, yet in the time of Seti the fine artistic traditions had hardly passed their height, and the work of his reign—of which a great deal remains—is in some ways as good as anything in Egypt, while the character of the man seems to shine through the distance of time and the dreary formality of Egyptian inscriptions with a rare nobility. The features of his blackened mummy can hardly fail to inspire reverence and cause us to regret that the bodies of these great kings of the old world should be laid out in museum cases like any ordinary curios. It is much to be hoped that the time is not far off when they may be more fitly shown.

Think of the resting-place Seti made for himself! His coffin, carved out of a single block of creamy alabaster, is still to be seen in a small London museum in the house of Sir John Soane, where it is the chief object of interest. It was taken away from the tomb by Belzoni in 1817 and eventually sold. If we can in thought replace it in the funeral chamber, far down at the end of his deep rock tomb, among the strangely beautiful shapes of gods and men and demons that decorate the walls, and lay again in the coffin the dead king, wrapped in fine linen and covered with royal jewels, we gain some idea of the burial that such a king thought worthy of him. It is fair to say that it was not at the hands of modern robbers, scientific or otherwise, that the mummies of most of these kings were taken out of their tombs; indeed, it was probably not by robbers at all, but by pious men of later times who hid them away in a place of safety to escape the devastation and sacrilege imminent from some foreign invasion. The often told tale of the finding of them in 1881 need not be repeated here; it is rather our business to think of them as they were in their glory and to try to fit together the evidence which shows us their works in life and their preparation for death.

Seti's grave is visited by everyone who goes to the Valley of the Tombs of the Kings, and most people stop on their way to look at his funerary temple at Gurneh, where throughout the dynasty the worshippers of the deified Seti must have carried on their services in his honour. Perhaps it ought to be noted here that the old principle of two parts being essential to a grave still held good, although it was no longer necessary that they should be in close proximity. A precipitous ridge of lofty cliffs separates the royal tombs of the New Empire from the mortuary temples on the edge of the desert, but these temples were no less devoted to the glory and the worship of the kings who erected them than were the ancient temples of the pyramids of Sakkara and Giza.

Seti made at least one very successful expedition into Syria; there he reconquered a great part of the country and re-established Egyptian naval bases for the fleet at certain of the coast towns. He needed to import a great deal of material from Syria for all the work he had in

mind to do, and he required vast quantities of gold to
pay for his imports and for all his building and repairing
in Egypt. The Sudan had always sent gold to Egypt,
and probably in early times this had been fairly easy to
work, but long before Seti's reign it had become necessary
to go farther afield and to carry on more and more extensive mining operations. It now meant a journey of many
days through the desert, and the difficulties caused by
want of water had become almost prohibitive. Seti went
out in person to explore the desert routes, and ordered
wells to be dug at any possible points and maps to be
made of the routes leading to the mines.

One of these maps, drawn on a sheet of papyrus, is in
the Museum of Turin; it is the oldest map in existence,
but there is, of course, every reason to suppose that maps
were made long before this time, for the Twelfth-Dynasty
engineers could certainly not have carried out the work
they did without pretty accurate surveying.

The mines in Seti's time were worked by prisoners,
not only the distant gold mines, but also the stone
quarries, and an inscription on the rocks at Silsileh tells
how very well they were treated in the matter of food and
clothes; they had plenty of bread, vegetables, and roast
meat daily and a clean suit twice in the month. It is
refreshing to come upon any such details of daily life in
the arid waste of Egyptian annals, but, however much
we may wish for more such flashes of light on secular
matters, it is mostly by his zeal for religion that Seti is
known to us.

His temple at Abydos contains some of the finest and
best preserved decoration in the country, and it displays
a spirit of reverence for the remote past which has not
hitherto been so noticeable, although the fact that Abydos
was the cemetery of the oldest dynasties and the reputed
burying-place of Osiris no doubt accounted for its pre-
eminent sanctity, which was acknowledged by the whole
country. Many people actually made their tombs at
Abydos so as to share in the privileges of the sacred spot,
but the more usual custom was to send there a funerary

stela, as it were, to represent the deceased in the great cemetery, for to be buried at Abydos was a literal " going West." There is a gorge in the desert out beyond the royal tombs, into which the setting sun seems to sink at the end of his course, and this was to the Egyptians the very gate of the West—of Amentet—the place of the dead, " the land that loveth silence."

Nearest of all the cemetery to these portals of the West are the *mastaba* tombs where the early kings lie (Chapter II.), to whom later ages looked back as to beings of unearthly antiquity. The mound over one of them came to be specially hallowed by tradition as the grave of Osiris—it is covered to this day by the broken fragments of offering jars left there by pilgrims in Seti's time and afterwards. Seti built his temple for the worship of Osiris, but in it he made chapels in honour of the old kings, where their names are written and form one of the early sources for our knowledge of the beginnings of Egyptian history.

But Seti's devotion to Amen Ra exceeded even this, and the Hypostyle Hall at Karnak, the largest pillared hall in the world, is the monument he raised for his father Amen Ra, king of all the gods. It possibly may have been designed by Horemheb, but the columns and wall-reliefs are the work of Seti, completed by Rameses II.

The subjects of this wall-decoration are of great historical importance, and careful research is bringing out their special object of setting forth the triumph of Amen Ra, the rewards he bestowed on his son Seti, and the ceremonies of coronation, etc., which were celebrated in this temple. Seti added a cedar pole to the sacred barque of the god (or he may have made a new barque on a larger scale), and he certainly altered doorways and passages in the Eighteenth-Dynasty parts of the temple to allow for room for the procession carrying this sacred boat.

Pictures of this procession cover the walls of the granite shrine, the Holy of Holies of Karnak, where the sacred barque reposed, and although these pictures are a late restoration there is no doubt that they are faithful copies of the old designs.

There is not very much of Seti's in Cairo Museum except his mummy, but we have already seen his work as restorer on the stela of Amenhotep III. (p. 103), and similar signs of his care in replacing the damaged name of Amen on cartouches where it had been chipped out by Akhenaten are to be seen on several temples.

His son Rameses II. had a different spirit and seldom hesitated to appropriate to himself any work of art that took his fancy, but with all his faults the best work of his reign is very fine, and he must have been a marvel of energy. Whether or not Moses and Aaron ever stood before him or whether they had long ago gone out of Egypt is somewhat doubtful, but it does not need much imagination to see on the worn face of that man, nearly ninety years of age, who lies before us in his coffin, the features of an imperious ruler.

His statues and monuments, like his children, were extremely numerous. He is said to have had well over a hundred sons and as many daughters, and there are no Egyptian collections of any importance that have not one or more representations of him. A small quartzite head in the British Museum is a very beautiful piece of work. He was a great builder, too, and the best buildings, like the best of his portraits, are very good indeed. No one who has seen the temple of Abu Simbel, guarded by his four colossal statues, can fail to feel that in its solemn magnificence it is one of the masterpieces of Egyptian art, while his funerary temple at Thebes, the Ramesseum, is without doubt the most picturesque of all the long row of temples along the desert, but this is perhaps in some measure due to the condition in which it is of partial but not too complete ruin.

At Karnak Rameses II. finished the Hypostyle Hall, which his father had not lived to complete, built the forecourt of Luxor temple, and in addition to these immense works he did a great deal more in the Delta,

apparently, than any of his predecessors, for, while
Thebes remained the religious capital of the country,
Rameses and his successors tended to live more at Tanis,
the old Hyksos town in the north-east. Owing to the
extreme difficulty of excavation there, very little has
come out of Tanis, either belonging to Rameses II. or
to the preceding age, but Rameses certainly found and
inscribed there his name on the big black granite statues
and sphinxes which have been described as probably far
more ancient (p. 75).

Tanis was a more convenient centre for the capital of a
new empire, which Rameses hoped would include Syria
within its bounds, than Thebes ever could have been;
also the desire for a cooler climate may have entered into
this preference for the north, only at the present day the
water supply of Tanis is so bad and the situation among
salt marshes so unhealthy that some great change in the
conditions of the place must have come about since the
New Empire, in fact a general subsidence of that part of
the Delta is supposed to have happened in the early
centuries of the Christian era.

In one of the earliest of Rameses' many campaigns in
Syria he met with a great adventure, which he afterwards
described and pictured at length on the temple walls of
Karnak, the Ramesseum, and Luxor. The account of
the Battle of Kadesh against the Hittite king Metella and
his Syrian allies is a really graphic piece of literature,
and it does not at all resemble the usual conventional
accounts of their victories which we expect to find the
Egyptian kings writing out for the benefit of posterity.

The tale begins with the taking captive of two Arab
prisoners, who really were spies sent by the Hittite king
and gave false information that the enemy were retreat-
ing and had practically evacuated Kadesh and its neigh-
bourhood. Acting on this, Rameses pushed forward
rapidly with one division of his troops, and afterwards
left even these and went on with only his bodyguard,
believing that he had nothing to do but to march into
Kadesh. Then the Hittites fell upon this single division

and put it to flight, while the chariots gathered round
the town to cut off all chance of the king's escaping.
The first news of the disaster that reached Rameses was
from some companies of the defeated division who rushed
into his camp in disorder, and their evil tidings were
confirmed by two more captured Beduins, who con-
fessed, under the lash, that the King of the Hittites had
his whole army drawn up around Kadesh. There surely
must have been some extraordinary error on the part of
the Hittite commander, as there seemed absolutely no
chance for Rameses to get away, but in the face of this
terrible situation the young king behaved like a hero,
and, instead of surrendering, grasped the fact that in
boldness and lightning swiftness lay one possible way of
safety. He charged in his chariot at the thinnest point
of the enveloping line, broke it, charged again, and
drove back the King of Aleppo and his forces to the
river, where he held them until reinforcements came up.
It was not a victory for Egypt, but the marvel was that
he saved it from being a crushing defeat.

The representation of this Battle of Kadesh on the
temple walls of the Ramesseum and Karnak are well
known, but the vast composition was too much for
Egyptian artists, and the result is rather confused, not
beautiful, and very difficult to understand without the
help of a handbook, but those accustomed to Egyptian
drawing of scenes will be able to trace the line of the
river, the fortress, and the troops of the King of Aleppo
struggling in the water and some drowned in their flight,
while the king himself is being held upside down by one
of his rescuers, probably to let him get rid of the water
he had swallowed. The King of Egypt standing in
his chariot and charging his foes is, of course, unmis-
takable.

After this Rameses made a great many campaigns in
Syria, but the Hittite power was so strong there that he
never regained complete supremacy over the country,
and at the death of the Hittite king Metella he made
peace on equal terms with Metella's successor, Khet

Asar. A copy of the terms of this treaty was made by the Hittites on a silver tablet and sent to Egypt; there must also have been a copy made in Egypt and sent to the Hittites, but neither of these survives. The wording of the tablet, however, is known, as Rameses had it inscribed on the temple walls at Thebes, where it may still be read. This peace was kept during the remainder of Rameses' long reign. Some thirteen years later he married the daughter of Khet Asar, and the Hittite king came to Egypt to celebrate the occasion and to confirm the friendship. The foreign princess received the Egyptian name of Mut Neferu Ra and was considered as "the great royal wife," but had many colleagues in the dignity.

The queen, whose features are best known to us, Nefertari, who was already married at the time of Rameses' accession, is buried in the Valley of the Tombs of the Queens, and her figure often appears by the side of the king on his colossal statues in Luxor temple and elsewhere. The beautiful and very brilliant paintings in her tomb show a new experiment in technique, for an effect of modelling is given by shading on the face and arms. This also may be seen in some of the private tombs of the period.

Perhaps the best portrait of Rameses himself is in Turin, but the Cairo Museum has many of his monuments, and within easy reach of Cairo are one or two statues of him which are seen by all visitors who go to Sakkara from Bedrashein and pass over the Memphis mounds. There, in front of the temple of Ptah, he set up the two mighty colossal figures now fallen to the ground, and made other large additions to the old shrine, among them the sphinx with the royal head which was found and raised on to its pedestal a few years ago.

After a reign of sixty-seven years, and at the age of ninety, he passed away and left the kingdom to his thirteenth son, Merenptah, who was already well on in life, but inherited a goodly portion of his father's energy. He, too, erected temples and other buildings on an extensive scale, and was even more unscrupulous than his father in taking possession of monuments which were already standing.

Merenptah's name is widely known, largely because of the tradition that he was the Pharaoh who hardened his heart and would not let Israel go, but, as has been seen, this title to fame is at the least uncertain. As regards art, his reign is generally considered to mark a decided decadence, but there is much beauty in the portrait head of him on his granite sarcophagus, which lies in place in his tomb in the valley at Thebes, and also in his colossal portrait in Cairo Museum. His funerary temple was on the desert, just behind the temple of Amenhotep III., which he ransacked to furnish it, and here it was that the fine stela of Amenhotep of which the vicissitudes have been described at length (p. 103) was finally discovered, having been employed by Merenptah to strengthen his foundations. Another stela of Amenhotep III., which was also "annexed" by Merenptah, has still the original Eighteenth-Dynasty inscription on one side, but on its other face Merenptah engraved a long list of his conquests. He conducted a great many campaigns, for there were revolts against Egypt both in Syria and on the western front, where the Libyans were beginning to exercise a serious pressure, and probably all that Merenptah was able to do was to hold Egypt and keep out invasion, but to that extent at least he did defeat his enemies on both fronts and made large claims to victory on his monuments.

This stela is particularly interesting, as in it there occurs the first mention in Egyptian of the people of Israel, of whom it is said, in a description of the state of Canaan : "They of Jenoam have ceased to exist, the people of Israel are laid waste and their seed is destroyed, Syria is become as the widows of Egypt." This passage, although perhaps not conclusive evidence against the Exodus having taken place in the time of Merenptah, is undoubtedly a serious difficulty, and would be much easier to understand under the other hypothesis, for in that case Israel would have been settled in Palestine long before.

Recent excavations have uncovered the ruins of a palace built by Merenptah at Memphis, not far from the temple of Ptah, with which it may have been connected. Some columns from this palace are in the Cairo Museum and show a curious decoration of coloured faience inlay, which was much used in the building. A great deal of gold leaf was also employed, and the general effect, even when toned down by a very subdued light, must have been extraordinarily gay—not to say gaudy. And at Abydos, behind the great temple of Osiris, there are large buildings, not yet entirely cleared and not at all well understood. They were certainly connected with the Mysteries of Osiris, which in some way showed forth his death and resurrection, but the nature of the ceremonies is quite unknown.

One or two long corridors are inscribed with cartouches of Merenptah and have every appearance of being his work, but a few years ago a building on a lower level and of a totally different character was unearthed. Its walls are of massive sandstone blocks, but it is divided into aisles by magnificent granite columns and architraves of a size exceeding those even in the Granite Temple; these are perfectly plain and supremely impressive. The sandstone wall at the eastern end is covered by inscriptions of Merenptah, but no one with any knowledge of Egyptian art could for one moment credit him with having designed or carried out such a building as this. As it is undoubtedly very like Chephren's temple in style, it is most probably of the same period, and may be considered as another splendid Old Empire edifice; but the possibility should not be lost sight of that it may be a solitary example of a great monument of the Middle Empire. No one visiting Abydos should fail to go round to the back of the temple and see this most imposing ruin.

The private tombs of the Nineteenth Dynasty are extremely interesting and show some novelty of treatment. The execution is generally much more rapid and free than in those of the Eighteenth Dynasty, and there is less regularity of arrangement of the scenes, for subjects concerned with the funerary service and the judgment in the other world now begin to appear on the walls of the outer chapel as well as of the inner part.

Graceful lines and pleasing colour are characteristic of this period : most visitors see the beautiful tomb of Nefertari in the Valley of the Queens, and the smaller tombs of Nekht, Menna, and Userhat, all on the way between the Ramesseum and Der el Bahri, are well worth a visit. Plate XIV. is interesting as giving an idea of how very excellently objects of daily life were made at this time. This silver vase with a golden rim and golden ibex as a handle was found some years ago in the rubbish mounds of Zagazig (Bubastis), together with a great quantity of jewellery and household and kitchen utensils. They probably came from a goldsmith's workshop, for the large numbers of some objects could have had no meaning in a private house, and, being found in the mounds of a ruined town, were, of course, intended for use in daily life and not as a provision for the tomb. The jewellery in this find is somewhat massive and heavy, less pleasing, perhaps, than the vases and goblets. All these objects are in the jewel room of Cairo Museum.

After Merenptah decadence fairly set in, and the Nineteenth Dynasty ends with a few rulers of little importance, of whom, however, there happen to be some relics in various museums ; but it is an obscure period and undoubtedly there were political troubles in the country. The army appears to have been strong, but was largely composed of foreigners who were at this time immigrating into Egypt in large numbers. Order was re-established under Setnekht and his son Rameses III., who may have been descendants of the old royal line, but assumed the titulary of a new dynasty.

CHAPTER X

LATE NEW EMPIRE: DYNASTIES XX.-XXVI.

(1205–663 B.C.)

RAMESES III. may be considered the last of the great Pharaohs of the New Empire. Not only did he, like his predecessors, rule with absolute supremacy over the whole of Egypt, but he carried his forces abroad, subdued Syria, and defeated the Libyans on the west. And he built as magnificently, if not quite so beautifully, as they had done, for his huge mortuary temple, Medinet Habu, yields to none of the others in size and splendour. It is the latest in time and the farthest to the south of all that rich array of pylons and columned halls that once edged the Theban desert. His tomb is in the Valley, a well-known one, with some good pictures of his foreign captives in it; his mummy and his shroud are in Cairo Museum. There exists, too, a papyrus which gives long lists of the booty he brought to Egypt and of his benefactions to the temple of Amen Ra, which exceeded anything done by his forerunners. The riches of Karnak and the amount of landed property possessed by the priests of Amen was enormous; in fact, the state of Egypt must have been something like what Italy was before the Risorgimento—the Church actually owned most of the land and drew dues and taxes from the royal estates as well.

Outside in the Mediterranean lands there was a changing world, for between the old Ægean civilisation and that of Greece and Rome there intervened centuries of barbarism; even as between the break-up of the Roman Empire and the rise of modern Europe, there lay the long gap of the "Dark Ages." It has been noted that in the time of Amenhotep III. or his son, some catastrophe overtook Knossos in Crete, which blots out its after history, and in the same way a shutter seems to descend on Troy, Mycenæ, and the other Ægean towns. The legends of their vanished courts and peoples are well known to us from the poems and plays of ancient Greece, where they represented the heroic age; the greatness of their art has come to us in recent years as a revelation, and it may be that further wonders will appear when their writings are deciphered, but, to present knowledge, all suddenly stops short and for centuries there is nothing to see, nothing to hear, except what Greek historians long after tell of the migrations, the wild northerners who came down to the southern sea and captured the mainlands and islands, harrying and destroying as they went.

In Syria a new, non-Semitic people, the Philistines, who were not there when the Children of Israel first got into the country, now appear in great strength. They are expressly said in some passages in the prophets to have come from Crete (Jer. xlvii. 5), and probably were emigrants from it and other islands, driven out under the pressure of the invading barbarians. It must have been from these civilised immigrants flying from their ravaged homes that the Semitic inhabitants of Tyre and Sidon learned their taste for trade and seafaring, and so carried on some measure of the old Minoan culture and traditions under what is known as the Phœnician Empire.

The illustration on p. 126 shows the head of a Philistine wearing the peculiar helmet by which they were distinguished. It comes from the temple of Medinet Habu.

Very likely more of these exiles from the Ægean are to be recognised in David's mercenary troops—the Cherethites and Pelethites.

On the inside and outside of the temple of Medinet Habu are many scenes of the king's victories and lists of the foreign towns which he captured, but the detail is rather coarse in workmanship and difficult to understand.

It is interesting, however, to notice how many foreign mercenaries Rameses III. employed, and also the fact that they are quite different in dress and type from the "foreigners" shown in the old Eighteenth-Dynasty tombs, and from the mercenary troops that took part in Rameses II.'s campaigns. These that occur most frequently on the walls of Medinet Habu are Sardinians and Philistines, but there are certainly others from among the many peoples who were wandering about at that time seeking new settlements.

PHILISTINE.

The two colossal statues of Amenhotep III. and Thyi, now in Cairo Museum, had been appropriated by Rameses from the temple of Amenhotep III. close by and set up in the Court of Medinet Habu. His palace was built adjoining the temple on the south, and a window may be seen in the wall of the temple where he used to appear to the people on state occasions from the palace. There are in the museum several windows and other architectural pieces from Medinet Habu and a fine series of figures of captives made of coloured faience from the inlay of a door.

For some five hundred years after Rameses III. there

are few outstanding events or figures in Egyptian history, but on the other hand a great deal is known about the period from the archæological side, and a picture can be formed of these centuries when Egypt was pursuing her lonely and pious ancient ways, while out of the chaos beyond her boundaries the forces were gradually shaping that were to bring about her overthrow. During the later Nineteenth and Twentieth Dynasties there is a notable change in tomb decoration in the direction of more elaborate mythology and funeral ritual. Scenes of the "weighing of the heart" and others which rightfully belong to the underworld, therefore to the interior of the coffin or burial chamber, now appear on the walls of the chapel. This weighing of the heart is a very frequent scene both in the Book of the Dead and on tomb walls. The dead man is led into the judgment hall by Anubis, who next appears as regulating the balances. In one scale is the heart, shaped like a little stone vase; in the other is the weight, in the form of a feather, the sign of truth. The weight is often made to represent the goddess Maat, goddess of Truth, wearing the feather as a head-dress. Above on an upper line are some of the figures of the deities who acted as jurors for Osiris; below a demon waits in case of an adverse verdict. Thoth, the scribe, writes down the confession of the dead man, which is spoken by his heart. Lastly, he is led into the presence of Osiris, Isis, and Nephthys and is pronounced "true of voice"—justified (see illustration, p. 128).

In this connection it may be well to mention a new use of scarabs which became common at this time. When the heart was removed from the body in the process of mummification, a large scarab was put in its place, generally made of black or dark green stone and inscribed with the chapter from the Book of the Dead relating to the "negative confession," so called because it consists of a long list of evil things that the man did not do, but the custom implies a rather high idea of personal responsibility. These scarabs are called "heart scarabs," and are well known in all collections.

A good example of tomb furniture of this time—in the Cairo Museum—is from the tomb of Sennejem, in the

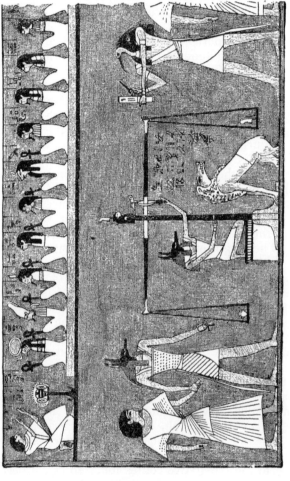

WEIGHING OF THE HEART.

same room as Ma her Pra's funerary outfit, which is about five hundred years older. The differences are striking.

Rameses III. was followed by eleven other kings, all

called Rameses, of whom very little is known except their tombs, but that little goes to show the ever increasing power of the priests of Amen Ra, and also the probability that order was no longer being very well kept. The priests were disquieted by rumours which reached them as to the state of the royal graves, and they appointed a commission to enquire into the matter. The report of this commission happily survives, and sheds much light on the legal procedure of the time. The witnesses were examined by beating, as would of course have been done in Egypt at any time before the English occupation ; and their evidence and subsequent inspection disclosed that a good many of the royal tombs had already been plundered.

Soon after this the feeble line of Ramesides seems to have died out, and the High Priest of Amen, Her Hor by name, took possession of the throne, uniting, as it were, the Empire with the Papacy. The kings of this priestly dynasty (the twenty-first), probably only controlled the south, for there were other kings ruling in Tanis, but they seem to have been connected by blood or marriage, and all to have been buried at Thebes. They were extremely pious in their devotion to the mummies of the kings, their predecessors; for instance, Her Hor rewrapped the body of Seti, Painezem that of Rameses II., and others were rewrapped even more than once, as the present linen shrouds bear testimony. They were so much concerned to keep the mummies safe from robbery that they moved them about and gathered several into one tomb to ensure better guarding ; finally a good many of the royal bodies were buried together in a vault near Der el Bahri, where they were found in modern times.

The coffins of these priest-kings themselves and their families were found in another *cache* near Der el Bahri, and form a series of much importance to the student of Egyptian religion, but they are so covered with detail that it is hopeless for anyone not a specialist to gather much meaning from them; the objects, however, which were buried along with them are of a good deal of interest.

9

This Twenty-first Dynasty was driven out by a stronger one, supposed to be Libyan in origin; the priest-kings fled, taking their learning and some of the treasures of Amen Ra with them, up to the distant Sudan, where they found a submissive people, already obedient to the spiritual and secular rule of Egypt, and they were able to carry on their religion and worship in peace and safety; and there, strange to say, they seem to have acquired new strength and vigour.

The Twenty-second Dynasty kings were mostly called Sheshonq and Osorkon and had their capital at Bubastis (Zagazig), where the ruins of a festival hall built by Osorkon II. for his " Sed Heb " or jubilee still exist. Although they had overcome the priestly dynasty which preceded them, they were still devout sons of Amen, and Sheshonq I. intended to build on a vast scale at Karnak; in fact he is believed to have laid out the huge forecourt, but he died before he had proceeded very far.   This Sheshonq I. is almost certainly the Shishak of whom we read in the First Book of Kings (ix. 16), that he captured Gezer and gave it as a dowry to his daughter on her marriage with Solomon.   He was no very good friend to his son-in-law afterwards, however, as it suited him too well that there should be quarrels in Palestine, and he gave shelter and hospitality to the two rival claimants to the throne of Israel, Hadad and Jeroboam, who had taken refuge in Egypt to escape from Solomon.   After the death of Solomon, Jeroboam was recalled by the Israelites, who were rebelling against King Rehoboam, and became the first king of the northern kingdom. Shishak came up to Jerusalem in the fifth year of Rehoboam, plundered the town and carried away the golden treasures of Solomon, and this campaign is recorded both in the Bible and on the walls of Karnak.

Artistically this is rather a dull period, and the amount of relics of it which fill many museums is perhaps responsible for the conventional ideas of art and religion which are associated with Egypt in the minds of many people, before they have seen the older monuments and realised how much more dignity and beauty the earlier art possesses. Here there are quantities of *ushabtiu* figures, Canopic vases, and elaborate coffins, painted with brilliant colours and decorated with scenes of worship and mythology repeated with wearisome iteration till all effect is lost.

At the close of the Twenty-second Dynasty we come on another of the obscure ages of Egypt, but light is just beginning to fall on it, thanks to recent researches in the far south. It has long been known that the Twenty-third Dynasty was reckoned as " Ethiopian " and that Egypt was governed from the distant capital of Napata, up at the Fourth Cataract of the Nile, but it comes as a surprise to find that this Ethiopian dominion was really Egyptian in the best sense; that its kings present themselves as guardians of Egyptian civilisation and traditions; that though their chief sanctuary was the temple of Amen at Napata, they were loyal worshippers of Amen at Thebes; and that under them art and literature flourished and were fresher and more vigorous than anything the Nile Valley had seen for generations. Dr. Reisner, of Harvard, excavating on behalf of Boston Museum, has in the last few years worked out the history of the Ethiopian kingdom in great detail. The kings reverted to the old Egyptian custom of being buried in pyramids; all of the pyramids have now been explored and identified with their builders, and Boston Museum has an extraordinarily fine display of the objects found in these royal graves and in the surrounding cemeteries. As the excavations are conducted by permission of the Sudan Government, the finds are divided between the Museums of Boston and Khartoum, and Cairo has no claim to them, but by arrangement with Dr. Reisner it has been possible to acquire a fine set of duplicates, mostly *ushabtiu* figures and foundation deposits from the pyramids, which are of great importance, as they fill in a period of Egyptian history from which, naturally, few royal monuments can ever be found in Egypt itself.

First and greatest among these Ethiopian kings is

Piankhi, whose exploits are inscribed on a stela found at Gebel Barkal, near the Fourth Cataract, many years ago. It shows that Egypt must have fallen to pieces at the end of the Twenty-second Dynasty, and that it was administered by local chiefs and nobles, all of whom owed allegiance to the Ethiopian king. It describes at some length and with quite unusual spirit, how Lower Egypt revolted and an expedition had to be sent from Nubia to subdue the rebels, how this army failed, and at last how the king himself at the head of his army made a victorious campaign. From the injunctions he gave to his troops as to how they should pay their devotions to Amen Ra as they passed Thebes on their way north, we see that he was at least as devout as any of his predecessors. He says : " When ye approach Thebes and the entrance to Karnak, enter ye into the water, wash ye in the river, dress on the bank of the stream, unstring the bow, loosen the arrow. Let no chief boast as possessing might, there is no strength to the mighty if he regard not Amen. He maketh the feeble handed to be strong handed; a multitude may turn their backs before a few; one man may conquer a thousand."

And afterwards, when Piankhi had finally overcome all the rebel princes and they had made submission to him, he went to the old temple of Ra of Heliopolis to give thanks for his victories and " entered the temple with rejoicings. The rites of the chamber of early morning were performed, the cloak was put on, he was purified with incense and cold water, flowers for the Hat Ben Ben (house of the obelisks) were brought to him. He took the flowers, he ascended the staircase to the great window to see Ra in the Hat Ben Ben. The king himself stood alone, he put the key in the bolt, he opened the double doors and saw his Father Ra at his rising."

One very pleasant touch in this fine inscription is his anger with Nemart of Heracleopolis for having let his horses starve. " As I live, as I love Ra, as my nostril is refreshed with life, very grievous are these things to my heart, the starving of my horses, more than any ill that thou hast done in the fulfilling of thine own desires."

But the Nubian kings soon had to face a harder task than the reconquest of Egypt. The rise of Assyria to a dominant place in the East had become a fearful danger to all its neighbours, for the Assyrians were the most cruel of conquerors. We read in the Old Testament how the cloud darkened over Syria, and it was only too sure that the rich land of Egypt would not long escape attack. Shabaka, the son of Piankhi, sent an army against them under Tirhaka (Taharka) which was defeated, but the mysterious destruction which overtook the army of Sennacherib at the gates of Jerusalem doubtless saved Egypt also for a time.

When Taharka succeeded to the throne he moved his capital down to Tanis in the Delta, hoping thus to be better able to hold the frontier of Egypt. He met Esarhaddon, King of Assyria, in battle several times, but generally got the worst of it, for though he managed to keep the south free from invasion, Memphis and the Delta were thoroughly pillaged by the Assyrians. This was quite a different thing for the country from being under a Libyan or a Nubian king, who had the same religion and customs as the Egyptians; the Assyrians were destroyers and plunderers, who sought only booty and carried death and devastation to every place where they penetrated. Taharka died and was safely buried in his pyramid in the Sudan, with treasures of gold and silver about him, some of which escaped the ancient robbers, and will be the glory of the museum at Khartoum, but in the reign of his son, Tabatamen, an attempt by the Delta princes to shake off the Assyrian yoke was crushed with appalling vehemence by Assurbanipal (Sardanapalus), who pushed up as far as Thebes and sacked it with a completeness of which we read in the prophet Nahum : " Art thou better than populous No [*e.g.*, No or Nut Amen—Thebes], that was situate among the waters, that had the waters round about it, whose rampart was the sea, and her wall was from the sea ? Ethiopia and Egypt were her strength, and it was infinite ; Put and Lubim [Upper Egypt and Libya] were her helpers. Yet was she carried away, she went into captivity : her young children also were dashed in pieces at the top of all the streets : and they cast lots for her honourable men, and all her great men were bound in chains." What riches Assurbanipal must have found there ! What golden store must have gone to fill the palaces of Nineveh ! What treasure of statues and beautiful columns must have been shattered and destroyed ! For Karnak had never before been plundered and its wealth must have been like the strength of Thebes—infinite. The Assyrians did not go farther south, and many Egyptians must have escaped to the remote capital in the Sudan, where they found a home among friends and kindred, and could worship their own god, Amen Ra, in their familiar way in his southern shrine. Egyptian art and religion flourished there for centuries, and only gradually assumed a more African character, as, with the rise of Egypt to power again under the Twenty-sixth Dynasty, its centre shifted to the northern parts of the Empire.

No attempt was made by the Assyrians to keep permanent hold over Thebes and Upper Egypt; after the sack of the place they went down stream again, and Thebes, though sorely fallen from its former glory, did not cease to be looked on as the religious capital. The high priestesses of Amen belonged to the old royal family and were closely related to the reigning kings in Ethiopia. It seems that they were looked on as the official wives of the god, so that it is not surprising that the succession, together with the right to the revenues of the temple, should have been vested in them, and that they were considered as the channel of the royal descent, which could now be transmitted by adoption. Thus Piankhi caused his wife and sister, Amenardas, to be adopted by Shepenuapet I., high priestess and daughter of Osorkon III. of the Twenty-second Dynasty. Amenardas is well known from a beautiful alabaster statue in

Cairo. Amenardas in turn adopted Shepenuapet II., the sister of Taharka, who was afterwards, when a very old woman, compelled by Psamtik I. to adopt his daughter Nitocris, and so to legitimise the new dynasty (the twenty-sixth), and at the same time transfer all the revenues belonging to the office. A stela exists with an account of this adoption which gives lists of the property held by the high priestess. The amount was still very large in spite of the recent destruction of so much of the temple treasure. The policy of these Theban princesses was guided by "the fourth prophet of Amen, Mentu-em Hat," whose wise old face is well known from his portrait in Cairo, a remarkable piece of work, showing great individuality. He administered their estates and did his utmost to repair the havoc wrought by the Assyrians.

During this very troubled time, when Thebes and Ethiopia were struggling to maintain independence, the Delta remained under the heavy yoke of Assyria, and when this was at length lightened by the pressure on Assyria by Medes and Scythians, Lower Egypt was once more divided up into petty principalities under local chiefs. In the Sudan, after the Twenty-sixth Dynasty, the separation from Egypt became gradually more marked; the capital was moved south from Napata to Meroe, south of Khartoum. This distant kingdom was practically independent of Egypt, and worked out a language and an art of its own, some of the products of which are remarkably interesting. For centuries longer the Ethiopian kings were still buried in pyramids, which, however, were very different from the old ones, being quite small and steep. There are traces of a female line of rulers at a late period. Probably "Candace, Queen of the Ethiopians," was one of these; in fact, Candace seems not to be a personal noun, but a royal title like Pharaoh.

CHAPTER XI

THE SAITIC PERIOD: PART I.—TWENTY-SIXTH DYNASTY

(663–525 B.C.)

FROM this time onwards the history of Egypt is so much involved with that of other nations that any short account of it is necessarily extremely incomplete; yet an attempt at fuller explanation demands so much space and leads us so far from the Egyptian monuments that the temptation to stray must be sternly resisted. It was noted in the last chapter that Egypt, while subject to Ethiopia, had been conquered by the Assyrians, who overran the Delta and pushed up the Nile as far as Thebes, which they sacked, but afterwards withdrew from Upper Egypt, which remained under the control of the Ethiopian dynasty.

The Books of Kings and of the Prophets are full of the events which were taking place at this time, for the position of the peoples of Palestine was perilous in the extreme; in fact, whether Egypt or Mesopotamia became conqueror in the struggle they were pretty certain to fall victims, and the prophecies are largely made up of warnings to Israel and Judah of the fate awaiting them in the near future and the not less certain vengeance that would overtake their enemies in time to come.

In the West, meanwhile, out of the confusion of migrating peoples, a new order had shaped itself, and on the mainland of Greece, the islands, and the Asia Minor coast, a new civilisation was rising of a type the world had not yet seen. It was a dawning of a new day for the world when—

" Some grave Tyrian trader, from the sea
Descried at sunrise an emerging prow.

*   *   *   *   *

And saw the merry Grecian coaster come
Freighted with amber grapes and Chian wine,
Green bursting figs and tunnies steeped in brine,
And knew the intruders on his ancient home,
The young, light-hearted masters of the waves."

The Greeks brought a new breath of freedom, a new curiosity about the world, a new desire to lay down laws of right and justice for all mankind. Individual cities were developing institutions of their own and, though there was great rivalry between the states of the European and the Asiatic shores, all acknowledged and took pride in their common Hellenism. Greek thought and customs had begun to exercise much influence on the non-Hellenic states of Asia Minor also, while far west, on the banks of distant Tiber, a little community had just begun to try experiments in self-government which led to mighty results. But as yet Greek art was in the period we have learned to call archaic, and " classical " Greece—much less Rome—was not.

The weight of tradition lay too heavy on Egypt for her to be much affected by this change of outlook, but with the Twenty-sixth Dynasty she entered into regular relations of commerce with her neighbours to the east and west and began to admit strangers within her boundaries.

The Assyrian expeditions to Egypt had really been raids on a large scale, for the Assyrians never attempted to administer the country themselves, and the Delta was ruled by local chiefs, as it had been under the Ethiopians, only now they were obliged to pay tribute to Assyria and even to fight against the armies from Ethiopia which endeavoured to deliver them from the foreigners. In one of these battles, Necho, prince of Sais, was killed, and his son, Psamtik or Psammetichus, fled to Assyria, but was recalled after the Ethiopians were finally defeated. The account of the rise of the Twenty-sixth Dynasty under him is given by Herodotus, perhaps somewhat poetically, but certainly on the exact lines of what happened. He relates that the Delta was divided among twelve kings who ruled on terms of exact equality and the strictest friendship (perhaps a poetic touch here !), having made an agreement to that effect by reason of an oracle which had predicted that "whoever of them should offer an oblation in the temple of Vulcan (Ptah of Memphis) from a brazen bowl should reign over all Egypt." In course of time, on one occasion when the kings were about to offer their usual oblation, the high priest of Vulcan by mistake brought out eleven golden bowls instead of twelve, and Psamtik, without any evil intention, took off his brazen helmet and made the libation from it; but the other kings, seeing at once the significance of the act, resolved to put him to death; this sentence was, however, commuted to banishment to the marshlands of the northern Delta. When in exile he sent to Buto, to consult the ancient oracle there, and received the answer that "vengeance should come from the sea when men of brass should appear." He was incredulous that such a thing could happen, but when, after no long time, some Ionian and Carian pirates landed in Egypt, all clad in brazen armour, Psamtik, perceiving that here was the accomplishment of the oracle, offered them a high price for their assistance, and by their help, along with that of a party of Egyptians who were friendly to him, he gained the sovereignty over the whole country.

And from this time onwards the Greeks have come to Egypt to stay. No military expeditions could be undertaken without the aid of Greek mercenaries, and very soon the enterprise of Greek merchants claimed settlements and privileges within the boundaries of Egypt which had hitherto so carefully shut out all foreigners. They were, of course, allotted special districts, where their customs would not interfere with those of the Egyptian people; the soldiers were given two Delta towns as colonies, and the merchants got a quarter in Memphis, to begin with, and later were allowed to build

a new town for themselves at Naucratis in the Delta.
All this period, from the beginning of the Twenty-sixth
Dynasty, 663 B.C., down to the end of the Thirtieth
Dynasty in 330 B.C., is known as Saitic. The royal
residence was now at Sais, but there was a great deal
of building at Memphis and other towns, while Thebes
continued to be a sort of religious capital as well as the
chief sanctuary of the South. Very little survives of the
additions made at this time to the temple of Ptah at
Memphis, but one of the best known things in Egypt is
the Serapeum at Sakkara, where the largest and finest of
the immense bull coffins were the work of this time and
give some idea of the honour that must have been paid
to Apis in his lifetime when such vast expense was gone
to for his funeral. Ptah was believed to be incarnate in
a bull; the calf was selected by special markings and
was housed in the temple and treated with the utmost
reverence. One of the great sights of Memphis was to
watch him frisking about in his open courtyard, and his
movements were supposed to have oracular significance,
which was interpreted by the priests.

But the most marked feature of Saitic art and religion
was a revival of the past. It was a regular Renaissance,
and the admiration of the Twenty-sixth Dynasty Egyptians for the work of their ancestors of 2,000 years before
is something like the awaking of Europe in the sixteenth
century to the beauties of Greek art and literature.
Priesthoods were revived at the pyramid temples which
had been abandoned for so many ages, restoration and
repairs were extensively carried out, the old formulæ of
the tomb inscriptions were introduced, and the style of
the Old Empire sculptures was copied on the tomb
reliefs. In these and in many other ways the Egyptians
of the Saitic period tried to imitate their long perished
past, but it was all imitation and always shows itself.
No art can repeat itself after 2,000 years, and the gap
that separates Psammetichus from Khufu is not less than
that but more, and it is not by the archaistic wall-reliefs,
charming though they sometimes are, that Saitic art will

live, but by its own excellence in portraiture and in the great skill of goldsmiths and metal workers.

There are some interesting specimens of reliefs from tombs of this period in Cairo Museum, and the fine collection of bronze statuettes is of great importance by reason both of their artistic and their mythological significance. They are often figures of special divinities, such as Neith, the patroness of Sais, whom the Greeks identified with Athene, or the Osiris, Isis, and Horus triad; but also very frequently they are composite, one figure having the attributes of Amen Ra, Bes, Pasht, Khnum, and many others. This can only signify a growing belief in the real divine unity underlying all the forms in which divinity is expressed; and this idea, as well as the extraordinary skill with which they are treated, saves them from what would seem to be inevitable grotesqueness.

Another feature of this period is the great number of fine glaze *ushabtiu* figures, but here at the first glance a change is to be noted, for instead of little servants carrying their tool bags on their backs and their hoes on their shoulders, these figures are now mummy shaped, they have a flat band down the back, generally inscribed, and the hoe on the shoulders has been transformed into the crook and lash of Osiris; in fact, they are now figures of Osiris, although still intended as servants for the deceased. It is not quite clear to what difference in belief this corresponds, but the fact is evident.

Private burials were as rich as ever, and a few unrobbed tombs have shown the extreme care taken in mummification and bandaging. The contents of a small case in the jewel room all came from one mummy and form a very interesting collection of amulets, most of which were actually folded into the wrappings on the body. The style of the Saitic jewellery is very easy to recognise; it is exquisitely delicate and dainty, but lacks in some way the beauty of design of the jewels of Aahhotep from Thebes or of the Middle Empire princesses who were buried at Dahshur.

The history of this dynasty is known mostly from Herodotus, supplemented by Egyptian annals and by the books of the Old Testament. Herodotus visited Egypt not very long after the end of the Twenty-sixth Dynasty, and probably had good sources of information, for all discoveries and contemporary documents corroborate his accounts for this period, though for the early history he is manifestly unreliable.

Psammetichus I., who reigned fifty-four years, was a man of great talent and vigour and brought Egypt back to a position of high importance among the nations. He spent many years in consolidating the government of Egypt, in restoring temples and re-establishing the state religion; we have seen, too, how he legitimised his family, and at the same time utilised the revenues of Amen Ra by causing the high priestess of Amen, daughter of the old Ethiopian line, to adopt his daughter Nitocris. To the last, Psammetichus did not interfere with Ethiopia, but towards the end of his reign he planned an expedition into Palestine, which was carried out by his son Necho. This is what we read of in 2 Kings xxiii. 29 and 2 Chronicles xxxv. 20 to xxxvi. 4 : " In his time Pharaoh-Necho king of Egypt went up against the king of Assyria to the river Euphrates : and king Josiah went against him; and he slew him [Josiah] at Megiddo." Necho did not cross the Euphrates, but on his way back through Syria he laid Jerusalem under tribute and took away the king, Jehoahaz, to Egypt.

Soon after this came the fall of Assyria, for Nineveh was taken by the Babylonians under Nabopolassar the father of Nebuchadnezzar. They, helped by the Medes, soon overran all Syria, and Necho sent a second army to meet them as far as Carchemish, but it was severely defeated and, as the Book of Kings says, "' the king of Egypt came no more out of his land " (2 Kings xxiv. 7).

But Necho had meanwhile built a big navy with the intention of using the coast towns of Syria for his base, as had been done by the Eighteenth and Nineteenth Dynasty kings of Egypt, and when he had to give up this object of ambition, he turned to even larger schemes of foreign exploration. Herodotus speaks of him as having made the canal which connects the Nile with the Red Sea, "which Darius afterwards finished." It is certain, however, that there was a canal long before his time; it doubtless was repaired and deepened by Necho to allow of the passage of his large ships, and after it was finished, according to Herodotus, he employed his fleet to sail round Africa. The description of this is worth quoting, as the statement made—which was incredible to Herodotus—that during part of the voyage they had the sun on their right hand, is exactly what carries conviction to us that they really succeeded in sailing round the Cape of Good Hope. "Libya shows itself to be surrounded by water, except so much of it as borders upon Asia. Necho, King of Egypt, was the first who proved this; he, when he had ceased digging the canal leading from the Nile to the Arabian Gulf, sent certain Phœnicians in ships, with orders to sail back through the Pillars of Hercules . . . and so return to Egypt. The Phœnicians accordingly, setting out from the Red Sea, navigated the southern sea; when autumn came they went ashore and sowed the land, by whatever part of Libya they happened to be sailing, and waited for harvest; then having reaped the corn they put to sea again. When two years had passed, in the third, having doubled the Pillars of Hercules, they arrived in Egypt and related, what to me does not seem credible, but may to others, that as they sailed round Libya, they had the sun on their right hand."

An expedition was made by Necho's successor, Psamtik II., into the Sudan, which has become famous through a record of it which remains to this day on the leg of one of the colossal statues of Rameses II. before his temple at Abu Simbel. It consists of a few lines of Greek, written by one of the Greek soldiers with the army, to say that his company had been there, but it is one of the earliest Greek inscriptions in existence, and it is written in the manner known as " boustrophedon "—

backwards and forwards as a plough is worked—which is very rare, and as Psammetichus' reign can be exactly dated to 593-588 B.C., it gives an important point for Greek epigraphy.

Apries—Pharaoh Hophra—comes next in order, and he is best known from the Prophecies of Jeremiah, for he was casting longing eyes at Palestine again, and the Jews were divided into parties, some of which favoured the Egyptian, some the Babylonian alliance. It was with rooted and well justified distrust of Egypt that Jeremiah attached himself to the Babylonian side as being far the lesser evil of the two for his country, for Apries was not able to do much more than stir up rebellion against Babylon, which brought down a speedy retribution, and when Jerusalem at last met its doom at the hands of Nebuchadnezzar he offered a refuge within the borders of Egypt to such of the Jews as were able to escape. This refuge was in a Delta town where a Greek garrison was stationed, Daphnæ, as the Greeks called it, or Tahpanhes, as we know it in the Old Testament.

" If ye wholly set your faces to enter into Egypt, and go to sojourn there; then it shall come to pass, that the sword, which ye feared, shall overtake you there in the land of Egypt." It is not known how much of this prophecy was literally fulfilled, but Nebuchadnezzar did send an army against Egypt, which certainly came as far as the Egyptian border and probably a little farther, so, as Tahpanhes lay very near the frontier, it may well be that it fell to the forces of the King of Babylon and that the sword which they feared did actually overtake them in the refuge that they sought.

But the end of Babylon itself was not long deferred, and the tale of Belshazzar's feast and the sudden assault of the Medes is given us in most dramatic form in the Old Testament.

Apries began to have trouble in Egypt, before the end of his reign, with a military revolt which appears to have ended in his defeat and murder by Amasis, who had a large army under him. It would seem, from

Herodotus' account, that Amasis obtained the throne rather as a national leader of the Egyptians than as a commander of the mercenary troops; if so, he probably had some claim to the title of king which is not recorded, but there is no question as to his capacity as a ruler; indeed he had a great reputation beyond the boundaries of Egypt for wisdom and sagacity. He was the Amasis who gave to Polycrates of Samos the celebrated advice to throw away his ring, which is embodied in a ballad of Schiller's; and another of his friends was Crœsus of Lydia, the tale of whose greatness and downfall pointed a moral to schoolboys of Greece and Rome and has come down as a familiar story to us all. In his time Athens was already well on the way to her highest renown under the laws of Solon, which had taken the place of the earlier and harsher code, the older temples were rising on the Acropolis, Pisistratus was expelled, and Miltiades had gone to be tyrant of the Chersonese.

But before the end of Amasis' prosperous reign of forty-four years, a new peril had arisen in the East in the shape of the Empire of the Medes and Persians which had arisen on the ruins of Babylon and Assyria and was soon to overspread, like a mighty flood, the whole of the civilised world. Amasis was fully aware of it and did all that was possible in the way of alliances to guarantee himself, but in vain. He died before the storm burst over Egypt, but one by one the states of Asia Minor succumbed, and under Psamtik III. Cyrus victoriously invaded Egypt and established himself and his successors as the Persian Dynasty.

PART II.—PERSIAN RULE

(525–332 B.C.)

The Persians were conquerors of quite a different stamp from any that had gone before, and their conquests had a far greater element of stability. Theirs was indeed an oriental despotism, as the Assyrian had been, but they were not a Semitic people, and possibly on that account had more in common with the West. In their earlier days, at all events, even their enemies acknowledged their many admirable qualities, and the Persian type of character appealed strongly to the Greeks, for whom in turn the Persians had enormous admiration. Their military power was very great, and after the conquest of Mesopotamia and Egypt, one after another the countries of Asia Minor, both the Asiatic states like Lydia and the Greek colonies on the coast, fell to them. It is the eternal glory of the two or three little states that formed European Greece that they withstood all temptation to yield to a foe who would by no means have been a cruel master, but whose victory would have been the death-blow to freedom.

The Persian rule in Egypt lasted from 525 B.C. down to Alexander's conquest in 332 B.C., with an interruption of some forty or fifty years when a native Egyptian dynasty once more managed to expel the invader and make Egypt independent. During those two centuries the type of art which is called Saitic went on with very little change. The Persians paid great deference to the gods of the country, even restoring and rebuilding in their honour. It was in their time that the temples in the western oases were built; one of these, at Kharga, is one of the most complete and best preserved in Egypt.

Herodotus' visit to Egypt took place at this time and he was very deeply impressed with what he saw, not merely with the great art of the Old Empire but also with the Saitic temples at Memphis, Sais, and other places. To us, looking back, with a better knowledge of the history than Herodotus was able to acquire, Egypt seems by the Persian period to have descended far on the path of decadence, and we cannot but remember how more than 2,000 years had passed since the age of the pyramids and the statues and paintings of Memphis, and how nearly 1,000 years had gone since her highest flight of thought had been cut short by the early death of Akhenaten. But Egypt, with all the massive splendour of temples full of worshippers, and long processions of priests and people, dressed in their clean white linen robes, passing through the streets, must have been a wonderful sight, and Herodotus, coming from Athens, then at her highest glory with Phidias, Sophocles, and Æschylus at work, could still say of Egypt that "it possesses more wonders than any other country and exhibits works greater than can be described in comparison with all other regions."

He was quite aware of the great age of Memphis and Heliopolis, but naturally saw more of the Saitic temples of the Delta, none of which now exist except for a few fragments in some of the remaining mounds.

Cambyses, the son of Cyrus, was the first Persian king of Egypt, and one of the few records he left is to be seen on a small Apis coffin in the Serapeum at Sakkara; he is more often remembered by a dreadful outrage committed on the sacred bull during a fit of the insanity which seized him. He is said to have killed the Apis and to have scourged the priests of Ptah of Memphis. But these acts were prompted by blind personal folly, they were no part of the Persian policy; and with the accession of Darius the well-being of Egypt came into the hands of a most enlightened sovereign. Herodotus speaks of him as having "completed the canal between the Nile and the Red Sea which Necho had begun," but, as we have seen, there is every reason to believe that the canal was in full use in the time of Necho, so Herodotus' statement can only refer to works of repairs or enlargement.

The Persians came as deliverers to the Jews everywhere, and an interesting sidelight comes from Egypt which shows their very favourable attitude to the Jewish settlers there. These had probably come in as a military colony and had been settled with their families at Assuan, where they had a temple and a regular ritual like the Jews at Jerusalem. This is a matter of recent discovery, from a find of papyrus on the Island of

Elephantine, which contains a number of documents of great importance. The papyri are written in Aramaic and relate that the temple was sacked by a band of Egyptians from Kom Ombos, whether from hatred of the Jews and the foreign religion, or simply in hope of plunder, is not clear, but it happened at a time when they might very well have thought they could get off with it, for the Persian Satrap, who was Viceroy of Egypt, was away on leave and it was very difficult for the Jews to get any redress. However, the Jews were not discouraged, and resolved to send their case to the official who was acting for the absent Governor. They had a long way to send, for this official was the Satrap of Samaria, and was no other than Sanballat of whom there is much mention in the Book of Nehemiah. He found judgment for the Jews, and condemned the people of Kom Ombos to rebuild the Jewish temple at Assuan, which they had destroyed, and to repair all other damage at their own cost. The letter, the copy of the letter, and the reply of the Satrap from Samaria, are all in existence.

A well-known group of tombs at Sakkara dates from this period and shows the enormous expense and labour which were lavished on graves in the hope that they might escape from the ravages which had overtaken those of past ages. These are generally called the " Persian tombs," but are simply Saitic tombs made in the Persian period.

Under Xerxes and his successors Persia began to have troubles nearer home, and had doubtless been weakened by the Greek repulse of their invading army. At all events, their hold on Egypt relaxed a little, and a series of successful rebellions under Egyptian leaders constitute the Twenty-seventh, Twenty-eighth, and Twenty-ninth Dynasties, but these were hardly independent of Persia. This is a most obscure part of the history, and it is only with the rise of the Thirtieth Dynasty under Nectanebo, a prince of Sebennytus, that Egypt really achieved again independence. That, indeed, was only possible by the aid of Greek mercenaries, who were by now employed by everybody. The Persian army could do nothing without them, and victory often depended on the number of Greeks which either side could afford to engage.

But, in spite of the cost of upkeep of a foreign army, the wealth of Egypt was so great that as soon as they had no longer to pay tribute to alien masters and the resources of the country were properly managed, the Egyptians always had money to spend on buildings, and the Thirtieth Dynasty has left a surprising number of monuments.

In art it is indistinguishable from the earlier Saitic, the Twenty-sixth; there is the same dexterity in working enormous blocks of stone, the same lace-like detail of decoration on shrines and coffins, and the same very fine metal work. Large stone sarcophagi, both of royal and private individuals, are a feature of this period and are much prized in museums. They are generally made of black granite or basalt and covered with decoration that is almost like a lace pattern in fineness and intricacy. The British Museum possesses a considerable collection of these coffins, and is, altogether, rich in objects of the Saitic and Ptolemaic epoch.

The most remarkable of all, however, are the well-known sarcophagi of the Apis Bulls in the Serapeum of Sakkara, which bear witness that the phenomenal capacity of the Egyptians for handling and moving enormous blocks of stone had not by any means yet subsided.

The temple of Philæ seems to have been begun under this dynasty, and the two Nectanebos built extensively also at Karnak, Kharga, Memphis, and Sais. In Cairo Museum there are some remarkably beautiful shrines and statues as well as splendid coffins of black basalt. Among these, the small coffin of a dwarf, with his figure carved on the lid, has the peculiarity that the figure is drawn in perspective instead of in the conventional Egyptian way; perhaps it was felt that such a distorted and grotesque little body could hardly be shown in the orthodox manner and must be treated naturally. The inscription on the sarcophagus tells that he was a dancing dwarf and danced at the funeral of the Apis Bull.

The figure of a certain Psammetichus under protection of the Hathor cow is much admired, and so are a series of bronze statues of gods which continues from the Twenty-sixth Dynasty, and in which a new element now begins to appear—the worship of Isis and Horus as mother and child, and also of the Child Horus as distinct from his worship as Sun God. The Osiris cult altogether came more and more to the fore during these later Egyptian dynasties and perhaps some forms of the Osiris myth took on new developments. A large figure of the dead Osiris from Abydos is interesting as illustrating part of the myth of his resurrection.

Under Nectanebo II. Persia gathered again a large force of Greek soldiers to march against Egypt. Assisted by treachery from within, the Persian army took Pelusium, then Memphis; Nectanebo fled to distant Ethiopia, where Egyptian tradition and religion were still reverenced; Egypt fell back under the dominion of a foreign foe and never again did a king of Egyptian blood bear rule over her.

These new Persian conquerors were of a different breed from Cyrus and Darius, and for the next few years Egypt suffered fearfully under them. They cared for nothing but plunder, and wantonly destroyed most of the temples as a revenge for what they held to be the revolt of Egypt. They were worse in deliberate destructiveness than Cambyses had been in his madness, for they killed and banqueted off the Sacred Apis and the Ram of Mendes, and destroyed and ravaged temples throughout the length and width of the land. But Egypt had not long to wait for a deliverer.

CHAPTER XII

ALEXANDER AND THE PTOLEMIES

(332–31 B.C.)

WHEN Alexander the Great set out to conquer all the world there was one power and one only that had any force to oppose him. This was Persia, for at that time the Persian Empire extended far beyond the boundaries of Persia and Mesopotamia and embraced Asia Minor, Syria, and Egypt.

He first encountered the army of the King of Persia at Granicus, soon after he had crossed the Bosphorus, next at Issus in Cilicia, then he marched on southwards through Syria, where he wanted to secure the coast towns so as to have a safe naval base. It took him seven months to reduce Tyre and two for Gaza, but he did not have much trouble anywhere else, and when he advanced on Egypt he was hailed as a saviour and a deliverer from the dreadful oppression of the last Persian conquerors.

There was much in the history and religion of Egypt that was sure to appeal strongly to Alexander's imagination, and especially he saw, in the literal acceptance by the Egyptians of the divine parentage of the king, an idea that exactly suited him and fitted in with his conceptions of a world-wide Empire. So he was ready to go far beyond what Darius, the former noble and enlightened foreign ruler of Egypt, had done : Darius had honoured the gods of Egypt and had built temples for them, but Alexander would become one of them, even as the kings of old had been.

So he took counsel with the Egyptian priests, and with their help and advice he planned out the manner in which he should be acknowledged as the son of the Sun

God, and it was in accordance with this scheme that he carried out his famous journey to the Oasis of Siwah, where the oracle of Zeus Amen had its seat. It is not known why he did not rather go to Thebes and be acknowledged there in the ancient shrine at Karnak; perhaps the Holy of Holies at Karnak was in too terrible a condition of ruin at the hands of the Persians to admit of the ceremony necessary, or possibly he wished to impress the Greek world with his divinity, for this oracle, placed as it was between the Greek state of Cyrene and Egypt, had great authority among them.

He took the old literal Theban form of the tale of his descent, for though the story only exists in late versions, the writers of which were ignorant of the Egyptian belief, it is easy to see that it must originally have run as follows : The last of the old line of kings, Nectanebo, instead of escaping to the Sudan from the Persian invasion, as was currently believed, had fled to Macedonia, where he became acquainted with the mother of Alexander, and as, long before, in the guise of the absent husband, the god Amen had visited the mothers of Hatshepsut and Amenhotep III., so now, having taken the appearance of Nectanebo, a lover, the god became the father of Alexander and predicted to Olympias his mighty future.

We may conjecture that Alexander's tutor Aristotle, and a good many of his friends in Greece, must have looked on this elaborately manufactured myth with very much the eyes that we do at the present day, but however that may have been, Alexander himself was delighted with it and must have considered that it added immensely to his glory in the world, for he regularly assumed the ram's horns of Amen as his head-dress on state occasions, and it is in this way that he acquired the title of the two-horned Alexander.

He went from Memphis to the Oasis by the long route down to the western or Canopic mouth of the Nile, and thence along the coast to the place now known as Mersa Matruh. Probably he took this way because he had the mind to found a new city which should have a fine harbour and should become a meeting-place for East and West and a trading centre for all the Mediterranean, in place of Tyre, which he had destroyed.

He saw the site he wanted on a narrow stretch of land between the sea and Lake Mareotis, and there, near a little village called Rakotis, he laid the foundations of Alexandria, which was to be for centuries the greatest town of the Hellenic world. After his visit to Siwah he came back by the desert route to Memphis, where he was crowned King of Egypt in the old temple of Ptah, and then, having made some arrangements for the administration of the country, he went off through Syria and farther and farther east until he met and overthrew an enormous army of the King of Persia at Gaugamela in the Euphrates Valley. After this his mastery was unchallenged, but his career was almost over. He celebrated the marriage of East and West as a step towards carrying out the fusion of which he had dreamed, but his death, at thirty-three, with no heir designated and no plans made for the government of his vast empire, threw all his schemes into hopeless confusion, and for years to come the world was torn between rival claimants for the succession to the different parts of his dominions.

His body was brought to Egypt with great pomp and is said tó have been laid for some time in a tomb at Sakkara, while the sumptuous mausoleum which was to be its final resting-place was being prepared at Alexandria. He is believed to have been buried in a golden coffin, which was afterwards replaced by one of glass, but nothing is known as to how long the body was preserved there or its subsequent fate.

One of Alexander's generals and most trusted friends had already his eye on Egypt as his future possession. This was Ptolemy, son of Lagus, a very able man indeed, of whose origin and early life little is known, but who succeeded in founding a dynasty—foreign, it is true, but the kings of which, by thorough comprehension of Egyptian ideas and customs, ruled wisely and brought the country once more to a state of extraordinary prosperity.

During the first few years Ptolemy only called himself Satrap of Egypt, first under allegiance to Philip Arridæus, Alexander's half-brother, who acted as regent, then under Alexander IV., Alexander's posthumous son, but after the death of the young Alexander he came forward in his own name as the founder of a new dynasty.

Ptolemy was acceptable on the whole to the Egyptians, who must have been glad to get a good government and a settled, civilised life again, and from the first he obtained much assistance and advice from the priests, in return for which he was most liberal in restoring the temples which the Persians had destroyed. The granite shrine at Karnak, the Holy of Holies in which the sacred Barque of Amen rested, was rebuilt by him while he was acting for Philip Arridæus, in whose name the work was done, and where the statue of Alexander IV., now in Cairo Museum, was found. The wall-reliefs on the outside of the shrine are almost certainly an exact reproduction of the ancient decoration and show the procession passing through the temple, the golden barque carried round by five rows of priests till it reposed again on the granite pedestal within the shrine; then the king himself entering in alone to the holy place, unfastening the bolt, and through the open window beholding his father the rising Sun.

The question as to how Ptolemy worked out a divine descent for himself so as to satisfy Egyptian theory is enveloped in mystery, but that he and his successors did consider it worth while to do so the family history leaves no doubt, and it seems likely that it was early decided that the succession should go to the children of Berenike, whom he married late in life and by whom he had a son and two daughters. Ptolemy and Berenike were worshipped together as the gods " Soteres," for Ptolemy gained the surname of Soter for benefits he conferred on the island of Rhodes.

An important innovation of his was the introduction of an Egyptian coinage. Coined money had been brought in by the Greek traders and used to a considerable extent long before this time, but the coins were foreign—usually the Athenian drachma, a silver coin about the size of a shilling, which was current round most of the Mediterranean countries.   Egyptian coins of Ptolemy I. are common.

Ptolemy " Soter " and Berenike were succeeded by their son Ptolemy Philadelphus, whose first wife and mother of his heir was Arsinoe of Thrace, but his second and far more famous consort was another Arsinoe, his full sister, some eight years older than himself, who had been left a widow after very tragic experiences.   It seems obvious that he must have married her for dynastic reasons entirely, and this is confirmed by the fact that she at once adopted the children of her predecessor, who quietly retired to Upper Egypt.   This, of course, shows that Arsinoe was assumed to have an equal divine right with Ptolemy and that adoption by her was necessary to give Ptolemy's son full title to the throne, but the marriage of brother and sister, though, as has been seen, of frequent occurrence in Egypt, was viewed in Greece with much the same abhorrence as it is looked on to-day among ourselves, and gave rise to much scandal.

Ptolemy, however, evidently thought that his business was with Egypt and that he could afford to disregard Greek criticism; in which he was probably correct, for his wealth and the great inducements the Court of Alexandria had to offer were enough to attract around him a most brilliant company of literary and scientific men, the poet Theocritus among the number.

It was his policy to make Alexandria the most magnificent city and the greatest intellectual centre in the world, and to his father and to him were due the foundation of the great Library and Museum, the temple of Serapis and the Pharos, which was reckoned among the wonders of the world.   It stood on the promontory where is now the Fort of Kait Bey, and many finely-dressed blocks of stone from the great lighthouse remain visible where the waves wash round the rocky shore.

The building has totally disappeared, but its appearance is more or less known from the descriptions of Arab historians who regarded it with the deepest admiration. It was built not only to be a guide to mariners, but to report the approach of ships coming into port, for in the open lantern which formed its top storey was a wonderful mirror, which flashed the rays of the sun by day and its own beacon fires by night for many miles out to sea, and in which approaching or departing ships could be seen from a great distance.

The Pharos is said to have been 300 cubits (about 500 feet) in height, and was built in four storeys, all of finely-hewn white stone. The ground floor was square, the second octagonal, the third circular, and the topmost an open dome which contained the mirror. The plan of building a high tower to give light was continued by the Arabs, and the design of the four storeys, decreasing in size towards the top, can be traced even in the elongated, slender minarets of modern mosques, but much more clearly in some of the older buildings, such as Ibn Tulun.

Great scientific knowledge as well as manual skill must have been required for the making of such a mirror as that described, but in almost all branches of science the Alexandrian Greeks were far ahead of the Europeans of the Renaissance, as the works of Euclid, Galen, and others show, while the scientific spirit was as much alive as modern education could desire. There must, of course, have been many first-class works of art at Alexandria also, but hardly anything of its treasures has survived, and the Greek pieces in the museums of Alexandria and Cairo are mostly of second or third rate quality. A few small bronzes and terra-cottas in Cairo are attractive, but on the whole ancient Alexandria has so completely disappeared that we are in constant danger of forgetting what a very important place it was and what a large part it played in Hellenistic history. Egypt and the Nile lay, as of old, unchanging, rich, and mysterious, but Alexandria looked out to the Western Sea and gathered men and manners from every part of the known world into its cosmopolitan society.

The great Arsinoe, Ptolemy's sister and wife, whose features are well known from a very lovely gold coin, is specially associated with a large scheme of irrigation by which the province of the Fayum was added to Egypt. It may be remembered that part of the Fayum had been reclaimed under the Twelfth Dynasty, but the Ptolemaic engineers undertook a very much bigger piece of work, by means of which the area of the lake was much diminished and a huge tract of very valuable land was drained and cultivated. This was afterwards known as the Arsinoite nome or province, and was granted to retired soldiers—Greek mercenaries—who were thus induced to settle in Egypt in considerable numbers. The Fayum was reckoned to be the best ground in Egypt for fruit growing, especially for vines and olives, and it continued to be highly prosperous until late Roman times, when the irrigation works were no longer properly kept up, the towns became mounds of dust and sand, and the place gradually became absorbed by the surrounding desert.

But out of these dust-heaps left by the old towns, from the gleanings of the rubbish that was buried there, the world has learnt within the last few years an immense amount about the working of government in Ptolemaic and Roman times; from receipts torn up and thrown away the prices of commodities and the system of credit can be understood, and from old letters and drafts of wills and deeds much of the habits of life of the ordinary citizen has become familiar to scholars, who can tell us how much pocket money a schoolboy was allowed and how a dinner invitation was worded, as well as the more important matters of complaints about the inspector of irrigation or the reclamation of taxes. Precious scraps, too, from the books these Greeks read have been found, bits of Homer and others of the known classical authors, new fragments of Sappho, some comedies of Menander, and works of other lost writers; best known of all, the page of papyrus on which was written a very early extract from some of the sayings of Christ—similar to but not identical with any recorded in the Gospels.

All the Ptolemies were very liberal to Egyptian religion, and restored and rebuilt temples all over the country. We are not, indeed, always ready to remember how many of the temples date from this (by Egyptian reckoning) very late period, which is generally talked of as one of deep decadence in Egyptian art. It is true that the decoration on the walls of the temples is very bad compared with the beautiful sculpture of ancient times, but the tradition of great building survived, and no one can fail to be impressed by the pillared halls of Edfu, a complete temple to this day, and one which bears special witness to the continuity of Ptolemaic policy, for almost every king of the dynasty added something to it. And Dendera, also complete, Philæ, Kom Ombos, Esna, Der el Medinet, were all built under the Ptolemies, not as new centres of worship, but as providing more sumptuous shrines for the gods of the land in their old sanctuaries.

The eye wearies of the mechanical workmanship, the rounded, high relief, and the monotony of pattern in all this temple decoration, but some of the scenes are interesting enough in themselves, for recent research has brought out the fact that the rites performed in any special part of a temple were, as far as possible, depicted on its walls, as when, for instance, we see a procession of figures on the walls of a corridor or staircase it means that such a procession did actually pass along it, and it appears that the grotesque figures of men with jackal and ibis heads are not symbolical figures of the gods, as used to be supposed, but simply masked priests who wear on their heads the image of the sacred animal, and thus act the part of the different gods who preside at the coronation and other festivals.

The texts on the temple walls are often very difficult to read, for the Egyptian language had by this time got into a highly artificial state. There had always been, of course, besides the formal decorative hieroglyphic script, a writing in cursive characters known as hieratic, which was used for all ordinary purposes and was, in old times, practically identical with the more elaborate inscriptions on tomb or temple walls.

As time went on, however, the popular language modified much more than the formal written Egyptian language did, and by the Saitic period the difference between the two was as great as that between the Arabic of the Koran and the spoken Arabic of the present day.

All the papyri of this time, accounts, letters, and even tales and romances, were written in the popular language, which is called demotic. The characters are usually very rapidly and rather carelessly made and are extremely hard to decipher, while the very late forms of words and difference of expressions make the study of demotic so hard that only a small number of scholars have as yet undertaken it.

Meantime the hieroglyphic script really had become a sort of religious puzzle understood only by the priests, who often manipulated it in fantastic ways, so that the Ptolemaic texts differ widely from those on the walls of the older temples, though, as it happens, they were among the first to be deciphered.

Two important inscriptions of this period gave the key to the Egyptian language, owing to their having a Greek translation appended. These are the Rosetta Stone, now in the British Museum, and the Decree of Canopus in Cairo. Both are written in hieroglyphics, demotic, and Greek. The Rosetta Stone was first read by Champollion, who, having carefully compared the cartouches in the Egyptian version with the royal names in the Greek, came to the correct conclusion that the hieroglyphics, instead of being symbols, as had been previously believed, were simply letters of the alphabet and syllables, and could be read like any other language. Afterwards, little by little, he recognised many words which still existed in Coptic, and thus was able in course of time to construct a grammar, which laid the foundations for subsequent study.

The Canopic Stone, which was found some years later than the other, formed a most valuable test of the decipherment already made and a triumphant confirmation of its accuracy. It is earlier in date than the Rosetta Stone and consists of a long inscription decreeing divine honours to a little princess named Berenike, daughter of Ptolemy III., who died young; incidentally it records the introduction of a leap year into the calendar.

The best Egyptian work at this time is a continuation of the Saitic style, and is characterised by the same love of hard, highly polished stone and intricate, lace-like patterns covering most of the surface, as seen on several of the basalt coffins in the museum. There are some interesting sculptors' studies in the Cairo Museum and many choice bronzes, among which are specially to be noted the large number of figures of Isis nursing Horus and of Horus the Child, or Harpocrates. This was the only cult common to the Greeks and Egyptians, for in Alexandria the worship of Serapis, a god of Greek origin, introduced for some as yet obscure reason by Ptolemy I., had superseded everything else, and there Serapis even takes the place of Osiris as the husband of Isis and father of Horus, though in the rest of Egypt he never became very prominent.

In the Cairo Museum are some good specimens of gold and silver work, both ornaments and services for the table, and some recently acquired objects are worth a good deal of attention. In the spring of 1918, peasants, digging for *sebakh* to put on their fields (p. 3), came upon a great treasure low down in the rubbish mounds surrounding the temple of Dendera, which forms another of the temple *caches* like that of Hieraconpolis (p. 11) or Karnak.

This dates from the late Ptolemaic period about 100 B.C., and though it is poor in workmanship must have been very brilliant in effect when seen in the dim light of an inner temple shrine. At the time of writing it has only been possible to show a few of the less fragile objects. Among them is a large figure of a hawk in silver gilt, the back of which lifts off and discloses inside the mummy of a real hawk, which had doubtless been one of the sacred animals of the temple when alive. Two others of these in less good condition were also found, and in all of them the bird was wrapped up with many amulets and covered with gold leaf. Besides these there are two statues of a young king or of Horus, two seated statuettes of a queen, all in silver gilt, a gigantic scarab of lapis-lazuli, and several other objects, the most important being a shrine of silver gilt with an inscription. No doubt these things were hidden away to avoid plunderers. It is not yet known at what time this may have happened, but by the end of the Ptolemaic period the country had in every way deteriorated to a considerable extent, and its internal history is rather obscure.

Under the first two or three kings it was a great and progressive state with a very liberal foreign policy. Ptolemy Philadelphus even sent an embassy far west to ask for the friendship of the young republic that was rising on the banks of the Tiber; the text of his message and the reply to it by the Roman Senate are given by Livy. And, true to this alliance, Egypt remained strictly neutral during the Punic Wars, and kept on good terms with Rome until the last days of the republic.

But the foreign policy of the later Ptolemies was almost entirely restricted to their relations with their neighbours in Syria, with whom they quarrelled and intermarried to a bewildering extent. Their domestic affairs were full of lurid and dramatic episodes, and the princesses of the family, the Arsinoes, Berenikes, Cleopatras, appear to have been women of remarkable capacity, gifted to an unusual degree both with talents and good looks.

Internally Egypt was prosperous and well governed until the reigns of the last two or three kings of the line, under whom, as has been said, a general decadence set in, irrigation works were no longer well looked after, and there was disorder in the provinces. The fact was that Rome already overshadowed the world, and by the time

of the last and most famous of the Ptolemies, Cleopatra
VI., the absorption of Egypt into the Roman Empire,
under one or other of the leaders who were fighting for
the mastery of the world, was a question of only a short
time. For a few brief years the full light of the world's
history flashes upon her marvellous figure, but in Egypt
she is little known. No likeness of her survives which
might have transmitted to us some faint idea of what her
charm must have been, for though she and Cæsarion—
her son and Cæsar's—stand figured in colossal size on
the walls of Dendera, the sculpture is of the dullest and
most conventional type. Egypt, indeed, was to her but
a pawn in her great game, which was no less than the
empire of half, if not all, the world. No doubt she must
have had great influence while Cæsar lived, for she
followed him to Rome from Alexandria and stayed there
until after his assassination, when she returned to Egypt
and associated Cæsarion with her on the throne.

Her second romance with Antony is too well known
and has been too superbly told to admit of comment here.
After Actium, when Antony's fall was certain, she seems
to have made an attempt to fascinate Augustus, and had
she been able to carry out that triumph over a third
victorious hero it would have been a most fitting culmina-
tion for all the traditions of her line and sequel to her
own past. But Augustus was cast in another mould,
and though he made some show of being charmed by
her, in the hope that he might be able to entice her to
Rome, where he would have the glory of showing her a
captive in his triumphal procession, Cleopatra was not
for a moment deceived into believing him to be in love,
and she saw that nothing was left for her but to die
grandly and dramatically. With her death Egypt ceased
to be an independent kingdom and passed, as Antony's
private estate, into the hands of Augustus.

CHAPTER XIII

ROMAN AND CHRISTIAN EGYPT

(30 B.C. TO A.D. 642)

THE history of Egypt as a Roman province is somewhat melancholy reading; there, as everywhere else under the Empire, the gods of the country were honoured and religious tradition observed, but when all the spirit that once animated Egyptian art and thought was dead so long, long ago, it is no wonder that the dreary repetition on temple walls of Roman Emperors dressed as Pharaohs and sacrificing to the Egyptian gods should fill us with a kind of disgust, and cause us to turn away from the empty forms of the State worship to see whether there was nothing better and more human in the everyday life of the Egyptian people. At first sight we are again disappointed and revolted by the ugliness of the objects of popular worship. Art had indeed sunk to a low level when the favourite ornaments of a household were the hideous little figures of Harpocrates, or Horus the Child, Bes and Isis, in terra-cotta, of which Cairo and the British Museum possess a fair, and Alexandria a large, collection.

From literature, too, we get a gloomy picture of Egypt. Juvenal's bitter satire, unfair though it may perhaps be, shows what the people of Egypt seemed to a Roman official who had to endure banishment among them, and nothing could be much worse than his description of their savage brutality.

Some of the practices of the popular religion, however, are by no means without glimmerings of a higher nature, while the burial customs begin to show an intermingling of foreign ideas with the ancient ritual which has a good deal of interest for us. There is in Cairo Museum a series of coffins with brightly coloured, almost gay masks, which certainly were inspired by Greek influences, while the other very well known " Fayum " coffins are of considerable importance in the history of art. The burial is Egyptian, the body mummified and wrapped up in the elaborate fashion of the late Ptolemaic period, but over the face a portrait of the deceased, painted on a wooden panel in western style, is let into the lid. These all come from the Greek colony in the Fayum, of which mention was made in the last chapter, and they are all pretty closely dated to the reign of Hadrian (A.D. 117- 138). There are a good number of these in European and American museums, and the National Gallery in London has two or three. Their importance lies in the fact that, with the exception of the Pompeian frescoes and one or two fragments in Rome, these are the only pieces of Greek painting in existence. Great Greek painting, like great Greek sculpture, doubtless flourished in the fourth and third centuries before Christ, and all the existing remains must be considered as belonging to a very late and decadent epoch, but as such, and as products of a country town in an obscure province, these portraits certainly surprise us by their excellence as well as by their curious modernity. The artists who painted them have more in common with Sargent than with Giovanni Bellini, with the twentieth century than with the fifteenth (Plate IV. 4).

In Cairo Museum there are, too, a few fairly good Græco-Roman bronzes and terra-cottas, and in Alexandria a rather larger collection, but singularly little of real merit.

Yet Alexandria at this time must not be reckoned with the rest of Egypt. Meagre as are its remains it was the greatest city of the East and one of the most beautiful in all the world. There seems to have been a subsidence of a large part of the Delta during the early Middle Ages, so that in Alexandria and elsewhere the walls and foundations of ancient buildings, systems of water pipes, and similar objects, are now far below water level and practically out of reach of excavations. A town, too, which is continuously inhabited for many centuries, and much disturbed by sieges and revolts during these ages, does not preserve much of its early character and it is extremely hard for us to restore in our imagination its former glories. An interesting passage in Butler's " Arab Conquest of Egypt " describes the effect on the invading Arabs of the sight of Alexandria : " Many of the soldiers in that army must have seen beautiful cities in Palestine . . . but nothing can have prepared them for the extraordinary magnificence of the city which now rose before them, as they passed among the gardens and vineyards and convents abounding in its environs. . . . Far as the eye could reach ran that matchless line of walls and towers which for centuries later excited the enthusiasm of travellers. Beyond and above them gleamed domes and pediments, columns and obelisks, statues, temples and palaces. To the left the view was bounded by the lofty Serapeum with its gilded roofs, and by the citadel on which Diocletian's Column stood conspicuous; to the right the great Cathedral of St. Mark was seen, and further west those obelisks called Cleopatra's needles, which even then were over 2,000 years old. The space between was filled with outlines of brillant architecture; and in the background, towering from the sea, stood that stupendous monument known as the Pharos, which rightly ranked as one of the wonders of the world."

Alexandria was no less famous as an intellectual and religious centre, and there is no doubt that some of the forms of Egyptian religion as practised there, that is to say, transformed in some degree by Greek habits of thought, had a very great influence in Europe, even in Rome itself—notably the worship of Isis and Serapis, to whom temples were raised in many Italian towns. Indeed, in the early years of the Roman Empire, there was much official talk deploring the introduction of " Eastern superstitions," such as the worship of Isis or Mithras; but, on looking deeper, we can hardly fail to see that these were just the beliefs that would help to satisfy the craving for a religion of the spirit for which the world was waiting. In Isis, the tender mother nursing her child, or the faithful goddess wife, who follows lamenting over her dead husband and afterwards shares with him the immortal life to which he rises, there was something more to fill the hearts of suffering men and women than they could find in the worship of the deified Roman Emperors, however excellently that might work as a State religion to bind together a great empire.

But before the Empire had been long established, and when Roman peace ruled from Britain to Assuan, from the Euphrates to the Atlantic, there took place the greatest event in the world's history—the birth of Jesus Christ. Nothing but late tradition can point out to us the spots that may have been associated with His stay in Egypt as a child—the tree at Heliopolis, the little crypt at Old Cairo, where the house of Joseph and Mary is said to have stood—but the religion which He founded spread very rapidly to Egypt, and there is good ground for believing that the Apostle Peter came there and wrote his letter to the Church from the Roman fortress of Babylon, now Old Cairo. And Mark, the beloved disciple of Peter, assuredly did come to Egypt, where he became the first Bishop of Alexandria, and from him in regular succession the bishops are named down to the present Patriarch of the Coptic Church.

The rise of Christianity in Egypt, its influence on the Christianity of the West and its unhappy isolation from the two great Churches of Europe are great subjects, far out of the reach of a little handbook like this, where we shall only venture on a few notes which may help to explain the Coptic monuments to be seen in museums. As Christianity spread in Egypt it had the effect, more strongly than anywhere else, of making its converts turn on their old religion with horror and loathing. The new Gospel gave them deliverance from bondage, and they could not break far enough away from the chains of their past. Everything had to be changed. Even their alphabet, and their written signs, the oldest in the world, were full of the forms of birds and beasts which they had ignorantly worshipped, and all must be discarded, for it was not meet to write of the things that pertained to the Lord God with the signs that had been consecrated to idols. In adopting the Greek alphabet, moreover, they were making a great advance in the means of expression, for Egyptian modes of writing were cumbersome and ill-suited for the conveyance of abstract ideas. So as Christianity was gradually adopted, the Egyptian language began to be written in Coptic characters, which consist simply of the Greek alphabet with the addition of seven letters to represent the sounds which exist in Egyptian but not in Greek.

Besides the writing, all else that savoured of the heathenish past had to go as well. Many are the signs in the rock tombs of Upper Egypt of what happened at this period of their history, when they were taken possession of by hermits who sought seclusion from the world in these desert fastnesses. And when the austerity of the anchorite took the form of defacing as sinful the lovely figure of an Eighteenth-Dynasty queen or goddess, it is difficult not to be as angry with the pious recluse as with the modern thief who chips it out for sale, though the motives of the two are such worlds apart.

Probably the earliest Christian churches in Egypt were built in Alexandria and within the enclosure of the fortress of Babylon, where the Roman garrison was lodged. The Nile at that time washed the walls of the fort and one of its gates opened directly on to the water. The flight of steps which led down to this gate has been uncovered of recent years, and it is known that a bridge of boats stretched across from it to the southern end of Roda Island, which was also strongly fortified. From very early times there were one or two churches inside the fort, and outside stretching gradually over the district now known as Fustat, there rose convents, churches, and other buildings attached to them. The new religion soon overspread the country and came into collision with the

State, for in Egypt, as elsewhere, the refusal of the Christians to sacrifice and offer incense to the statue of the Emperor brought them into trouble, and the Church suffered more or less serious persecutions, the worst of which, under Diocletian, A.D. 303, made so terrible an impression in Egypt that the Copts to the present day date their era from it instead of from the birth of Christ.

And after the Empire had embraced Christianity the troubles of Egypt grew worse rather than better, for now that the Church and State both had beliefs they really cared about, they came into constant instead of spasmodic conflict, for the Egyptian Christians somehow had invariably the bad luck to be opposed to the decisions of the Orthodox Church, while they were always ready to resort to force in support of their dissent. At the division of the Empire, under Constantine, Egypt fell to Byzantium with the rest of the East, and, as religious questions took a most prominent part in the subsequent history of Constantinople, the barque of the Church in Egypt was never out of storms. The Council of Chalcedon, which took place in A.D. 451, adopted, as the creed of the Church, the doctrine of the dual nature of Christ, but the Egyptian Church clung to the Monophysite position with intense ardour, and thereafter was considered to be heretical by the remainder of Christendom. This was a dreadful misfortune for the country, for an Orthodox archbishop, appointed from Constantinople, was henceforward the official head of the Church, but was absolutely rejected by the Egyptians, who appointed another archbishop or patriarch of their own persuasion, and the most violent quarrels ensued.

The old paganism was not quite dead; some fear of vengeance from the old discarded gods of ancient times certainly lingered among the country people, and in Alexandria, in the intellectual atmosphere of the Museum, there throve for a time the pure and refined philosophy which bore the name of Neoplatonism. But great as the influence of this school of thought may have been on some higher spirits of the age, it was not robust enough to stand against the furious religious bigotry of Christians and Jews, and in one of their vehement feuds there perished the beautiful and talented Hypatia, whose tragedy is so well known though its causes are obscure. She was probably murdered by way of vengeance against one of the leading Christians, whose friendship with the heathen lady had drawn down the anger of another faction.

Most of the history of this time is a horrible succession of fanatical brawls and feuds in Alexandria, while the monks and hermits who took refuge in the desert from the miseries of a distracted world have left such a picture of asceticism and such legends of self-torture and temptation that the one seems as far away as the other from the Christian idea of life. Yet, still, some of the greatest men of the early Church, Origen, Athanasius, and many more, lived in Alexandria and took part in its divisions, while the desert gave refuge to men like St. Jerome, who sought for peace and quietness to study, and to St. Benedict, who turned to Egypt to find a model for the communities he wished to found in the West.

For it was in Egypt that solitary hermits first grouped themselves into monasteries with an ordered rule, and some of the establishments they founded endure to this day, such as the Monastery of St. Anthony and St. Paul overlooking the Red Sea and the monasteries of the Wady Natron, where church bells have called to service day by day for sixteen centuries. The foundations of the White and Red Monastries at Ekhmim and of St. Simeon at Assuan go back to a very early period, but the principal Coptic monuments to be seen in Cairo date from the reign of Justinian and a little later (A.D. 500-700), and come from the ruined monasteries of St. Jeremias at Sakkara and of St. Apollo at Bawit in Middle Egypt. Some good pieces from the Monastery of Jeremias are in New York. West of Alexandria, and some fourteen or fifteen miles from the sea, a remarkable site was discovered in recent years by a German priest, the Abbé Kaufmann. It proved to be the sanctuary of St. Menas, whose legend is a picturesque one. He was a soldier in the Roman Army, was martyred for his faith, and his body was carried by a camel farther and farther west till at length the camel stood still, and it was signified to the mourners following that this was the spot destined for his burial. Round the tomb of the saint buildings gradually gathered, a deep well was dug, and this lonely shrine became a famous place of pilgrimage. The ruins of a vast church remain, monastery buildings and a hospice for pilgrims; bakeries, a pottery, and, strange to say, a large bath establishment, which, considering that at the present day there seems to be no water within many miles, is significant of some comparatively recent geologic change. Not only did the pilgrims get the chance of a bath, but they also carried away a little of the water in small terra-cotta vessels, which are well known in many museums. They are a kind of flat bottle and have a figure of the saint between two camels moulded on the surface.

The church was rich in marble columns and capitals, all of pre-Byzantine type and nearer to classical form than most Coptic remains.

Memphis by this time was falling into decay, but still had a considerable population, and a fine church and monastery were built on the slope of the desert at Sakkara nearest to the town. Many stones for the building were taken from the old tombs round about, but for the first church and the oldest parts of the monastery workmen were probably brought over from Constantinople, for the grey marble columns which supported the roof are believed to have come from a quarry near there, and the designs of the capitals and friezes are purely Byzantine and are exactly paralleled by sculptures in St. Sophia, the churches at Ravenna, and other Byzantine cathedrals (Plate XV.). The change from ancient Egyptian art could not be more complete, and these objects are of extreme interest as showing the uniformity of archi-tecture and ritual in the fifth century over the whole Christian Church. The oldest of them are the best, but the native artists adapted themselves to the new style, and the fine decorative character of old Egyptian art is continued in many of the Coptic designs, and forms the basis of later Arab conventionalised scroll patterns. Plate XV. shows a splendid capital, probably from one of the four columns supporting the dome of the ancient Cathedral of St. Mark's at Alexandria. The basket-work design is often met with in Byzantine churches in Italy and elsewhere, but this and two similar ones from the same great church, which are now in the Museum of Alexandria, are perhaps the finest in existence. More usual are patterns of vine leaves, grape clusters, and adaptations of acanthus foliage. The paintings, like the sculpture, are Byzantine in type, but are far less pleasing. There are in Cairo some frescoed niches and other pieces which give a fair idea of the style and are interesting—as any painting of the date must be—but are not to be compared with the very beautiful stonework. Occasionally, it must be admitted, when the artist harked back to paganism for his subjects and tried his hand at the human figure, the results are rather grotesque, but the vine and acanthus leaf designs are most excellent models of their kind. Coptic embroideries and patterns in woven tapestry are very fine, but the Cairo Museum is rather poor in these compared with South Kensington and New York.

Less than a century after the death of Justinian, Egypt had fallen on very evil days. The Persians, under Chosroes, had once more conquered it and plundered extensively, though afterwards this was compensated for to some extent by the removal of the " orthodox " archbishop, so that for a few years the Copts were permitted to please themselves; but when Heraclius reconquered Egypt for the Roman Empire a still worse thing befell. Heraclius had conceived a grand idea of healing the divisions of the Church of Christ by bringing the opposing parties to a mutual understanding, and believed that a compromise could be effected by which their differences might be thrown into the background and their unity emphasised. In consultation with several of the leaders of the Church he evolved a new doctrine which should alike meet the views of those who held the nature of Christ to be dual, or those who, like the Egyptians, affirmed it to be single. This is known as the Monothelite, and it set forward the view that whether the nature of Christ was dual or single was a great mystery, but that without doubt there was but one Will, and on this basis it was hoped that both parties would find a ground of agreement. This, however, was far from coming to pass, perhaps because he made a most unfortunate choice in the man he selected to carry out, or rather to enforce, his new creed.

He appointed Cyrus, a man destined to be the evil genius of Egypt, as Viceroy and Archbishop at once, who had therefore the control of all the imperial forces, spiritual and temporal. He met with the usual opposition to be expected in Egypt at the outset, but instead of labouring to conciliate his opponents he seems from the first to have had recourse to severity, and always more and more severity till the unhappy people and Church of Egypt were tortured and persecuted as they had hardly been in all their previous history, and all in the name of the Emperor's attempts at reconciliation. And for ten long years the Coptic Church suffered thus, and though a few, naturally, were terrified into submission to the Archbishop, by far the greater number were faithful to their own beliefs.

But a change came at last for Egypt, and a dark day dawned for the Roman world with the rise of Mohammed and the onrush of his armies from the Arabian desert. It was in A.D. 622 that Mohammed fled to Mecca from Medina, in 627 that he sent letters to the Emperor of Rome and to the King of Persia and other rulers inviting them to become converts to his new religion, and in 632 that he died, having already seen his armies dominant in Arabia and successfully invading Syria. Only nine years later, Amr ibn el Asy, seeing the wealth and weakness of Egypt, divided as it was by religious strife and suffering under a detested government, crossed the frontier at El Arish and marched through the desert to attack it.

It seemed a rather desperate venture for the Arab troops, bold and hardy as they were, to march against a country defended by a large Roman army who held at least two fortresses of first-class importance, Babylon and Alexandria, with entire command of the sea and communications with the capital of the Empire, but perhaps Amr may have counted somewhat on assistance from the Copts, who might well be expected to feel that any master in Egypt would be better for them than a Viceroy from Constantinople, and that no oppression from foreigners of an alien religion could be so bad as that of a fellow Christian of a different creed. Probably, too, the Arab general had hardly realised the magnitude of his task until he got into Egypt, when it was too late to draw back, and he went forward with a magnificent confidence in himself and the divine mission of the followers of the Prophet.

As a matter of fact, though some of the Copts doubtless did help the invaders, it was not by their assistance, but by the disgraceful capitulation of Cyrus, who seems to have proved himself both incapable and cowardly as a commander, that Amr got possession of the fortress of Babylon. Cyrus was recalled by the Emperor to give an account of his action, and the reason for his defeat, but things in Constantinople were by that time in hopeless confusion; Heraclius was dead, his son and successor only lived a few months, and Cyrus was able to convince the feeble young Emperor who followed that in the interest of the Roman State the best course was to conclude peace and pay a tribute to the Muslim conquerors. He returned to Alexandria with this mandate for the betrayal of Egypt, but kept it quiet until he could slip away secretly to Babylon, where he concluded the negotiations with Amr. This treaty provided for the payment of a tribute to the conquerors, evacuation of the country by the Roman Army, and a pledge that no attempt at reconquest should be made from Constantinople. In return for this the Egyptian Christians were to be left in undisturbed possession of their churches and the practice of their religion, and this undertaking was probably pretty well kept for some time. But inevitably, as Mohammedan domination became more complete over all the East and Egypt became more isolated from Western Christendom, the Egyptian Christians fell into a position of inferiority and were subjected to a steady oppression with intervals of active persecution, and in the course of centuries large numbers of them adopted Islam.

Thirteen centuries more of Egyptian history remain untold and many of the most famous and beautiful monuments of Egypt are as yet unnoticed. But it is mainly the history of the town of Cairo, a new city with a new religion and an altered art; its records are in a different language and form a separate literature, its archæology has a special museum set apart for its study. It seems, therefore, that a handbook of ancient Egyptian art and history comes suitably to an end with the day when Amr Ibn el Asy marched his victorious Arabs into Alexandria.

INDEX

Billing and Sons, Ltd., Printers, Guildford and Esher.

PLATE I.

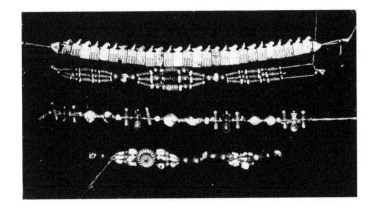

FIRST-DYNASTY BRACELETS.

See p. 16.

CEREMONIAL HATCHET OF KING AAHMES.

See p. 83.

EGYPTIAN HISTORY AND ART.

PLATE II.

MASTABA OF PERNEB IN METROPOLITAN MUSEUM, NEW YORK.

See p. 30.

PLATE III.

SARCOPHAGUS OF KHUFU-ANKH.

See p. 36.

PLATE IV.

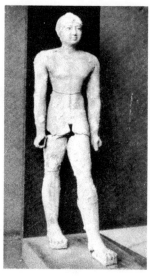

WOODEN FEMALE STATUE :
WIFE OF SHEIKH EL BELED.
See p. 39.

COPPER STATUE OF PRINCE
MEHTI-EM-SA-F.
See p. 47.

PORTRAIT OF THOTHMES III
See p. 92.

FAYUM PORTRAIT.
See p. 163.

PLATE V.

MUSICIANS. RELIEF FROM A FIFTH-DYNASTY CHAPEL.

See p. 43.

PLATE VI.

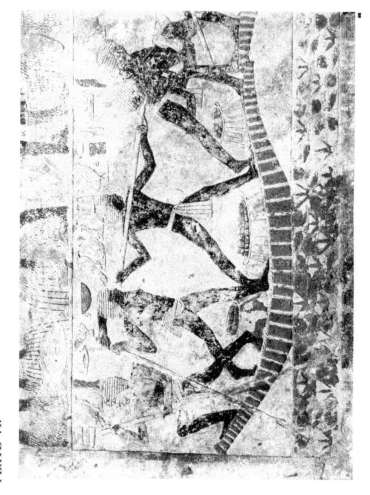

SCENE OF FIGHTING BOATMEN.   RELIEF FROM FIFTH-DYNASTY CHAPEL.

See p. 43.

PLATE VII.

SCENE OF CATTLE INSPECTION (ELEVENTH DYNASTY).

See p. 54.

PLATE VIII.A.

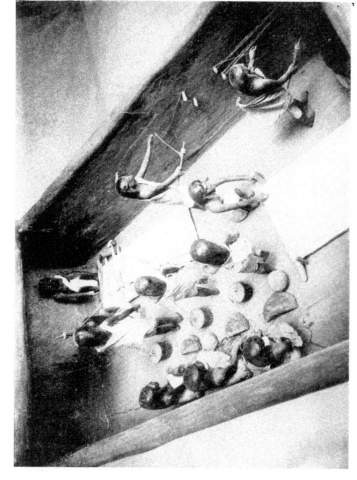

SPINNING AND WEAVING.

See p. 54.

PLATE VIII.B.

See p. 54.

MODEL BOAT.

PLATE IX.

MODEL OF DOMESTIC SCENE WITH MUSICIANS AND SINGERS.

See p. 54.

PLATE X.

QUEEN OF PUNT.

See p. 86.

LID OF CANOPIC JAR OF AKHENATEN.

See p. 105.

PLATE XI.

STELA OF AMENHOTEP III.

See pp. 103, 121.

PLATE XII.

STELA OF AKHENATEN.

See p. 105.

PLATE XIII.

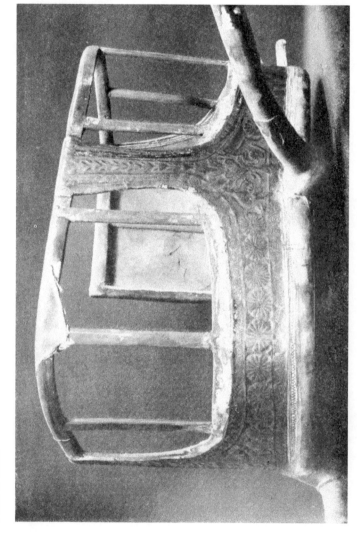

CHARIOT FROM TOMB OF YUAA AND THUAA.

See p. 99.

PLATE XIV.

SILVER VASE WITH GOLD HANDLE AND RIM.

See p. 123.

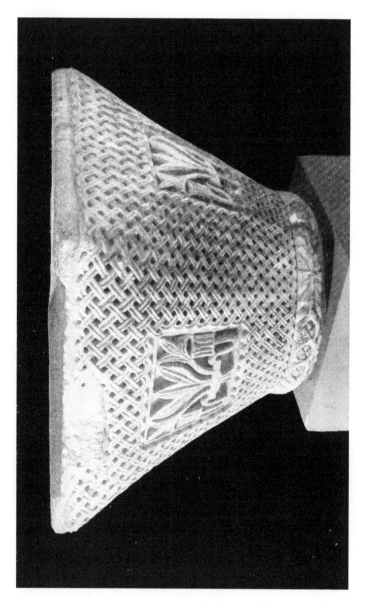

PLATE XV.

COPTIC CAPITAL.

See p. 170.

For EU product safety concerns, contact us at Calle de José Abascal, 56–1°,
28003 Madrid, Spain or eugpsr@cambridge.org.

www.ingramcontent.com/pod-product-compliance
Ingram Content Group UK Ltd.
Pitfield, Milton Keynes, MK11 3LW, UK
UKHW012346130625
459647UK00009B/579